Music Universe, Music Mind

Revisiting the Creative Music Studio,
Woodstock, New York

Robert E. Sweet

Arborville Publishing, Inc.
Ann Arbor, Michigan

Arborville Publishing, Inc.
P.O. Box 2767
Ann Arbor, MI 48106

Cover design by Hesseltine and DeMason
Ann Arbor, Michigan

Manufactured in the United States

LCCN 96-083108
ISBN 0-9650438-4-3

Contents

Acknowledgements

I am immeasurably grateful to all the musicians who gave life to this book through their enthusiastic reminiscences of the Creative Music Studio. Number one on the list is Karl Berger, who opened up the Creative Music Foundation archives to me, tracked down countless phone numbers, and gave the project his wholehearted support. The rest are too numerous to mention here, but they make themselves known throughout the pages of this book.

Even greater in number are the musicians whose stories do not appear. There were so many people from all parts of the globe who made the Creative Music Studio what it was; it was impracticable to even attempt to contact them all. Many were simply unavailable. And so, to all those who may feel slighted by their omission from this narrative, I offer my sincerest apologies.

Michael G. Nastos of WEMU radio, a National Public Radio affiliate in Ypsilanti, Michigan, made insightful, critical comments on the text. He offered suggestions that only he, with his singular knowledge of the world of creative music, could make.

My wife Gundy also put her skilled editor's eye to the task of making this book more readable. Her love, support, and forbearance throughout this whole project have been vital contributions, which have made it possible for me to carry through to completion.

For numerous and varied technical, textual, and inspirational contributions I'd like to thank Ilene Marder, Marianne Collins, Ingrid Sertso, Tom Schmidt, Larry Chernicoff, James Quinlan, Christy Bych, Kathleen Crockett Richards, and Betsy Folks.

The photographs in this book have been culled from the mass of negatives, contact sheets, and prints in the archives of the Creative Music Foundation, which has given authorization for their publication. Among the photographers who contributed to the Studio's ongoing documentation and who are known or believed to be represented herein are Raymond Ross, Alan Carey, Carolyn Schultz, Andrea Craig, Howie Greenberg, James Quinlan, Kathy Compton, Sylvain Leroux, and members of the *Woodstock Times* photographic staff. When possible, the photographers have been located, contacted, and their explicit permission to publish has been gained.

Preface

In January of 1976, I was playing drums in a bar band in Traverse City, Michigan. We were a quartet of musicians, all in our early twenties, who had had some instruction on our instruments, some experience in school bands, but were, for the most part, learning on the job, driven by our love of the music. Our repertoire was a standard sort of pop/rock/soul amalgam—Motown, Meters, Beatles, Tower of Power, Stevie Wonder. We even did Eddie Harris and Les McCann's "Compared to What" to let the people know that we were hip. But when I wasn't on the gig, I was drawn to, motivated by, and sustained by "the art of the improvisers."

The Detroit radio stations that had turned me on to Jimi Hendrix in the late sixties had also thrown a little Miles Davis and John Coltrane into the mix and set me on my way to discover jazz and the whole universe of improvised music. My musical guides became Miles, Coltrane, Art Blakey, Ornette Coleman, Olatunji, Charles Mingus, Albert Ayler, Ravi Shankar, Max Roach, and on and on. I had no loyalties to bebop, postbop, avant garde, fusion, cool, swing, Latin, or whatever. I soaked it all up. Communication technologies had brought the whole world of improvised music to my living room.

What happened next, for me, was the first of a number of episodes of near perfect timing—coincidences, if you will—that directed my life toward Woodstock, New York, and the Creative Music Studio Our quartet was breaking up, and I was ready for the next phase of my life, but without a clue of how it would unfold. I came upon a little ad in

7

Down Beat magazine, which was the first that I had heard of the Creative Music Studio (CMS). It was offering a chance to study music with some of the finest improvising musicians in the world: Jack DeJohnette, Dave Holland, Anthony Braxton, Ed Blackwell, Don Cherry, and a host of others whom I was at that time unfamiliar with, including Karl Berger. It seemed too good to be true. I had a car, a little bit of money, no commitments, and was faced with an opportunity of a lifetime. By March, I found myself transported from my humble rock-and-roll beginnings to a community of improvisers of the highest caliber.

I relate this episode because it is so similar to that of hundreds of other musicians from all over the world, who, by seeking a higher level (or is it a deeper level?) of musical expression, found themselves at the Creative Music Studio. Many were following commercial music careers; some were just discovering music; some already had university degrees in classical music studies; and some came with fully developed experimental concepts. They came from all levels of musical proficiency and from all backgrounds. All were welcomed with open arms. What we found at the Creative Music Studio was unique and it was amazing. There has never been anything in music education that could compare with the experience of CMS.

CMS was an environment in which personal expression was paramount. For some, there was too much freedom in that environment. For those of us who were open to the experience, our lives were changed forever. It was the type of experience that can make the rest of your life seem mundane.

The last CMS session that I attended was in the spring of 1979. Since that time, my life has taken many turns that have made Woodstock seem as if it were light years away. That heady, elevated feeling that comes from doing something truly extraordinary had become too much of a distant memory. Being at the Creative Music Studio had started to seem like a dream that I once had. That is why I decided to write this book.

I called Karl Berger, the director of the Creative Music Studio and the Creative Music Foundation, in the summer of 1994 and proposed to him the idea of a history of CMS. He was enthusiastically in favor of it. My wife and I then drove to Woodstock from Ann Arbor, Michigan, and I began a process of reconnection. By interviewing Karl and whatever remaining CMS people I could contact during our short visit, I began to reconstruct the rise and fall of this unique study center. Each person I spoke to was able to provide me with names and phone numbers of others who were involved. Over the course of a year and some months, I interviewed, by phone, as many people as I could reasonably contact. Musicians across the United States, in Canada, and Europe were eager to reminisce and relate their CMS stories. Their enthusiasm made my job much easier—a true labor of love.

Throughout the course of these interviews I became increasingly aware of a pattern of connectedness. It was often eerie, running into so many coincidences of time, people, and places. This emerging realization of my connectedness to a cultural phenomenon and the people who made it—a phenomenon much larger than I could measure by my own experience—convinced me of the necessity and the timeliness of recording what happened at CMS and attempting to place those events in the larger context of our arts, our society, and our times.

Many of the people interviewed I had never met. Others I hadn't spoken to in over fifteen years. Larry Chernicoff was one of those. I called Larry out of the blue one Sunday afternoon and he related the following incident. He and his daughter had been driving near his home in Massachusetts when they passed a sign advertising Pete Sweet's Tree Farm. They both found it amusing, and Larry told his little girl that he had known a guy named Bob Sweet at the Creative Music Studio. Not only hadn't he spoken to Bob Sweet since 1979, he probably hadn't thought about him either. Three hours later I called. A minor coincidence, perhaps, but typical of countless other personal connections that seemed downright uncanny.

Another series of connections, however, opened my eyes to the place that CMS holds in a larger, historical context of arts and education in the United States. While talking with Richard Teitelbaum, composer, educator, and electronic music innovator, he drew a parallel between CMS and Black Mountain College. His point was that if not for books like Martin Duberman's history of Black Mountain, the school probably would have fallen into complete obscurity.

He laughed when I told him that I had never heard of Black Mountain. "You see!" We agreed that it would be tragic if the Creative Music Studio were to be forgotten.

I didn't pick up Duberman's *Black Mountain: An Exploration in Community* until several months later. It was during a conversation with Doug Hesseltine, the designer of this book's cover, that a flash of coincidence struck me again, illuminating even more brightly this connection between Black Mountain and CMS. After I gave Doug some background on CMS, he told me how much it reminded him of Black Mountain College (BMC) in North Carolina. I knew, then, that it was time to look into Black Mountain.

When I began to read of the similarities and actual links between CMS and BMC, I was astonished. Karl Berger had told me that initial planning talks for CMS had included Buckminster Fuller, Willem de Kooning, and John Cage (whose CMS involvement I was vaguely familiar with), along with Ornette Coleman and others, and I was surprised at this range of notables from various artistic and philosophic disciplines. But here, in reading Duberman, I discovered that Fuller, de Kooning, and Cage were prominent figures at Black Mountain, teaching and developing some of their most important works there. The composer Christian Wolff also had taught and presented works at CMS and BMC. The similarities between the two schools (I hesitate to call CMS a school, but the term is useful for the sake of comparison) are undeniable. Both CMS and BMC were located in settings of natural scenic beauty, an aspect that lent much to their character; neither would have been what it was if located in a city. Both were controversial, inspiring acclaim and derision in students, locals, and observers of the arts. And both were established by German emigrants, followers of a school of artistic thought that would relentlessly draw its proponents to an environment of freedom so that it may be given expression.

Like Duberman, I found myself being affected by the place (he, BMC, and I, CMS) through the process of writing about it. He impressed me with his view that history is not actually served by separating the historian from the retelling; his willingness to insert himself into BMC's portrait gives his book a vitality and a warmth that might not otherwise be there. I am not a historian as is Duberman. On the other hand I was there. My frame of reference had already been laid; the interviews and the reacquaintance with CMS merely fleshed out a body of experience that had begun its evolution in 1976. My having been there and having been strongly and positively affected by the experience will no doubt lessen my objectivity. That's fine. It is not my aim to give an objective account. I wish only to give my own view, with the confidence that its corroboration by so many others who were there will give it legitimacy.

In an interview with the trombonist George Lewis, we touched on the difficulties of going about the process of defining improvisation—no easy task. It would require, George felt, an ongoing dialogue over a period of time among masters of the craft, in which various seemingly contradictory aspects could be examined and all individual interpretations could be given voice. We reached the conclusion that defining the importance of the Creative Music Studio or attempting to characterize what it meant to be there (the experience was so different for so many people), was equally daunting. George states that "at a certain point you say, well, here's my definition of improvisation right at the front. Well, maybe it's already a mistake. Maybe at this point, instead of defining, you just have cases, and then the cases add up to something. That's what I find about CMS. It's not like, aha, here's the epiphany which occurred while I was at CMS. It's more like, here are all these cases of encounters I've had with different people and what I learned from each one."

It is my hope that the encounters in this book, with the nearly one hundred musicians, writers, and administrators who participated in CMS on some level and who consented to interviews, will bring CMS into a clear enough focus that its contribution will be recognized and that its memory will endure.

Introduction

"The art of improvisation, in the foreground of contemporary musical practice, is an art of self discipline. Far from being a practice second to notated composition, it has been a means for even more precise personal expression in all the world's musical cultures, including the West. Studies of the world's musical cultures are to a large extent, studies in the art of improvisation; observations of attitudes and approaches are not merely interesting as exotic objects of study, but are directly inspiring as examples of this discipline. No matter what material one chooses to use today, this basic attitude of self discipline towards precision in all details must be developed.

The contemporary situation has created a new sense of the purpose and impact of the musical laws; a glimpse of what other cultures have known about the relationships of music to many areas of life. Basic musical training, the kind that does not deal with a particular musical style or with the playing of an instrument, seems to be beneficial for practically anyone. A sense of right timing and rhythmic cycles, for example, seems to be a basic human need. In fact, all the performing arts could benefit from these practices. This is why body discipline, dance, all visual media, poetry, songwriting are complementary to contemporary musical development." [1]

—Karl Berger

---

1. From a promotional brochure for the 1978-1979 Creative Music Studio sessions.

This book is about a unique endeavor in shared musical experience—musical education, yes, but so much more. The Creative Music Studio comprised an actual community in which music and the creative process were fused into a lifestyle that brought students of all levels into contact with seasoned, improvising professionals of the highest stature. The studio, founded in 1971, was located in a number of different sites in and around Woodstock, New York. And although there has been no CMS since 1984, the community that developed still exists in a remarkable network of creative musicians all over the globe.

There has never been another "school," or instructional musical offering of any type, that has brought together so many of the world's leading improvising or contemporary classical (or simply uncategorizable) musicians. The Creative Music Studio had a magnetic force that drew musical innovators from all over the world. By 1981, its tenth year, CMS had reached its goal of having better than 50 percent of its student body from outside the United States. Musicians came from Europe, Canada, Brazil, and Japan, as well as the United States. As the student participation became more international, so did the music. Guiding artists came from several countries in Africa, Europe, and the Americas, from India, Turkey, and Japan. The phenomenon of *world music*, whatever one considers that to be, cannot be fully examined without an understanding of what happened at CMS.

I will refer, throughout this book, to *students* and *teachers,* or *guiding artists.* Most musicians who were interviewed for this book, however, concurred with the idea that the line between student and teacher was frequently blurred. All who came were collaborators in studying, performing, and living music in an atmosphere that held personal expression paramount.

You will notice, too, that musicians are generally referred to by their first names. This is not done to appear overly familiar. This is done because that's the way it was at CMS, and I hope to portray realistically the intimacy and the extended-family quality that being part of this community provided.

Students had the opportunity not only to attend classes with the instructors but also to perform and record with them. During some sessions, students and instructors even lived in the same quarters, ate meals together, did laundry together, and in many cases forged ongoing professional relationships. The student-teacher interaction, in fact, was more like an apprenticeship. Much of the valuable learning came about through the experience of sharing life together, beyond developing the techniques of the craft.

14

In describing CMS, it's difficult not to compare the experience of going there with the experience of attending a university or conservatory's music program. When one thinks of music education, formal, academic environments are what naturally and most quickly come to mind. European classical music has been the standard, although many colleges now present programs in jazz studies. But there is actually no basis for comparison between CMS and traditional music schools, other than to say that there is music at each, and there is learning at each.

The closest thing to an educational experience of the sort that CMS offered would be an innovative jazz, world, or improvising music curriculum, such as those at the California Institute for the Arts, the University of Michigan, Wesleyan University, York University in Toronto, or the University of California at San Diego's Department of Critical Studies and Experimental Practices. However, none comes close. The Black Mountain College educational experience was similar in that it was a community of artists, living their art. But the music program there was just one component, and with the exception of John Cage's experimentation, it was presenting primarily the European classics. One way to convey the uniqueness of the Creative Music Studio is to present a list of the guiding artists. Some names are well known, others are quite obscure. You'll find dancers and poets in there, too.

John Abercrombie
Barry Altschul
Maryanne Amacher
Ramsey Ameen
William Ames
Derek Bailey
A. Spencer Barefield
David Behrman
Ingrid Berger (Ingrid Sertso)
Karl Berger
Ed Blackwell
Carla Bley
Lester Bowie
Anthony Braxton
Peter Brotzmann
John Cage
Baikida Carroll

Joseph Celli
Andrea Centazzo
Eugene Chadbourne
Don Cherry
Jay Clayton
Sara Cook
Jerome Cooper
Marilyn Crispell
Blondell Cummings
Alvin Curran
Z.M Dagar
Olu Dara
Anthony Davis
Donnie Davis
Thulani Davis
Jack DeJohnette
Paul De Marinas

Yaya Diallo
Robert Dick
Aiyb Dieng
Hamid Drake
James Emery
Douglas Ewart
Malachi Favors
Semith Firincioglu
Guillherme Franco
Becky Friend
Fred Frith
Paul & Limpe Fuchs
Allen Ginsberg
John Giorno
Jimmy Giuffre
Gene Golden
Andy Gonzalez
Jerry Gonzalez
Steve Gorn
Andre Goudbeek
Trilok Gurtu
Steve Haas
Charlie Haden
Mark Helias
Julius Hemphill
Dick Higgins
Gary Hill
Richard Hill
Anthony Holland
Dave Holland
William Hooker
Zakir Hussein
Abdullah Ibrahim
David Izenson
Michael Gregory Jackson
Ronald Shannon Jackson
Joseph Jarman
Ahmadu Jarr
Leroy Jenkins
Howard Johnson
Raymond Johnson
Rrata Christine Jones

Don Knaack
Steven Kolpan
Toshinori Kondo
Lee Konitz
Alhaji Bai Konte
Dembo Konte
Takehisa Kosugi
Peter Kowald
Garry Kvistad
Steve Lacy
Pheeroan ak Laff
Oliver Lake
Byard Lancaster
Jeanne Lee
George Lewis
Garrett List
Frank Lowe
Jimmy Lyons
Michael Lytle
Michael Mantler
Dumisani Maraire
John Marsh
Stu Martin
Kalaparusha Maurice McIntyre
Harry Miller
Roscoe Mitchell
Louis Moholo
Butch Morris
Bob Moses
Don Moye
Sunny Murray
Pandit Pran Nath
Babatunde Olatunji
Pauline Oliveros
Ursula Oppens
Peter Orlovsky
Gerald Oshita
K. Paramjyoti
Evan Parker
J.D. Parran
Hannibal Peterson
Henri Pousser

John Prienenger
Vasant Rai
Steve Reich
Sam Rivers
Roswell Rudd
Adam Rudolph
George Russell
Frederic Rzewski
G.S. Sachdev
Ed Sanders
Lakshmi Shankar
Schoenberg String Quartet
Alan Silva
Ismet Siral
Leo Smith
Harvey Sollberger
Speculum Musicae
Foday Musa Suso

Steve Swallow
Tamia
Cecil Taylor
John Tchicai
Richard Teitelbaum
Faruk Tekbilek
Haci Tekbilek
Yung Yung Tsuai
Erasto Vasconselos
Nana Vasconselos
Janine Pommy Vega
Murat Verdi
Collin Walcott
Ann Waldman
Carlos Ward
Philip Wilson
Gary Windo
John Zorn

This is an unprecedented and fascinating era. It is only within the last forty years or so that musicians have had, as a tool of their trade, the technology that can bring them musics that have originated in such a vast geographic and historic expanse. It is only within the last forty years or so that the world has become so small. Today, any musician with even modest resources can choose to listen to, study, and emulate the music of Duke Ellington, Mozart, Ecuadoran folk groups, Jimi Hendrix, John Coltrane, Tibetan monks, John Philip Sousa, shakuhachi or bansuri flute masters, Afro-Cuban drummers, Miles Davis, mariachis, Beethoven, Willie Dixon, or John Cage. Certainly there remain, and always will be, purists of style. But for the musician who is open to the universe of musical expression, it's all within reach.

The Creative Music Studio was not a place to come to learn how to play an instrument or to study any specific style. It was an environment in which musicians, regardless of their levels of proficiency, could give full attention to the universal elements of music and receive guidance from advanced professionals in developing a personal relationship with those elements. With a keener sense of what it really means to be in tune and in time, the individual is much better prepared to develop a freer, more personal expression within whatever musical context he or she chooses.

"We live in a Number One situation. Although we learn from traditions, we cannot simply continue them. They have been defined by world regions that have lost their exclusivity. We live in very transitional times. It is up to us what we make of them. . . .

Personal expression is now, more than ever, based on the discovery of personal potential and of personal tradition beyond tribal supports and securities. More than ever we must learn to start from the beginning, from the experience of silence, the experience of available space. Actually, that is an inspiring challenge, but not easy by any means. Personal discovery begins with the simple discipline of meditation, the meeting and making friends with oneself and the space around: centering oneself.

In search for our own music, we learn to realize that our personal material is already there, something to be discovered rather than learned. While we study our instruments and discipline our musical minds, our materials begin to surface. No one can teach anyone to play if the goal is improvisation. One can only teach common basics, awareness of the many details to be watched, traditional approaches, and try to be an example of some kind. Music is a lifelong study, a way of life. It begins by imitating others, sometimes almost to the point of total identification, the same way that children learn to walk talk and do things. This is an important period and not to be ridiculed at all. Certain inroads into personal aspects of music can only be made that way: understanding what the layers are that can be reached.

Finally, there can be the liberating experience that the material is not the point at all: We train ourselves to become instruments when the music can flow through freely, like electricity through a transmitter. We don't know where it is going. We don't even know what it is doing. We are only as ready as possible, keeping the tools sharp, keeping fine tuning— essentially empty so we can vibrate." [2]

—Karl Berger

---

2. This section of the 1978-1979 promotional brochure for the Creative Music Studio sessions was entitled "Liberation Through Sound."

Music Universe,
Music Mind

PART I

1

In the Sixties

"Any person in today's music scene knows that rock, classical, folk, and jazz are all yesterday's titles. I feel that the music world is getting closer to being a singular expression, one with endless musical stories of mankind."

— Ornette Coleman

Of all the individuals who have been credited with taking jazz music in entirely new directions, reshaping the music according to their own visions, Ornette Coleman is the only one still alive today. Hearing Ornette Coleman's music in the early sixties set pianist, vibraphonist Karl Berger in motion on his own musical path of freedom of expression. "When I first heard the Ornette Coleman Quartet," Karl recalls, "I guess that's when I decided to really be a jazz musician. That was the music that I wanted to play—just like that, free music that was rhythmical. That's still what I like best. Get that rhythm happening and play freely over it."

After finishing his doctorate in philosophy and music aesthetics in 1963 in Berlin, Karl returned to his home town of Heidelberg. There, in a little club called the Cave 54, he got the type of playing experience that was available only in New York.

One of the cultural benefits that the U.S. military supplied the area with was jazz. Heidelberg was surrounded by U.S. military bases and each base had a band. Karl remembers that "in those bands were some of the most famous jazz musicians—people who later became really famous, like Cedar Walton, Lex Humphries . . . Don Ellis . . . just a bunch of guys who came to the Cave every night. [Roscoe Mitchell of the Art Ensemble of Chicago met Karl there; Carlos Ward was also a regular.] So it was like growing up in New York."

Karl's love for the music of Ornette Coleman moved him to seek out trumpeter, multiinstrumentalist Don Cherry, who at the time was living and playing in Paris. "I had applied to write a book on music aesthetics in the West comparing it to the methods in the East," says Karl. "They gave me money to do that, and I could live anywhere I wanted to. So, we [Karl and his wife, vocalist Ingrid Sertso[1]] decided to go to Paris because Don Cherry was there. . . . I just went there. I knew I was meeting Don Cherry. It was a sure thing, a sure shot."

Karl has a determination and drive to make things happen that make him a master facilitator. So it's not surprising to learn that he and Don met the day that Karl arrived in Paris, and they were performing together the next night in the club where Don had been working. The two established a collaboration that continued and became one of the vital elements of the Creative Music Studio's personality. Don has called Karl "*the* pianist of the Ornette Coleman lineage."

Meeting Don Cherry was an important event in Ingrid's life also. It was Don who introduced Ingrid to the benefits, musical and personal, of Buddhist mental discipline. "Don was my spiritual brother," she states. "Don was a very powerful influence on me—the whole Ornette Coleman group, but mainly Don Cherry." It was actually a matter of meeting someone whom she felt very familiar with. "It was like meeting a long-lost brother. . . finding somebody who thinks and feels the way I do, without speaking it out."

"With Don we were in Paris for a year and a half," Karl recalls. "We had a club of our own to play called Le Chat qui' Pêche. It was a very different situation. . . . There we played every night except Mondays. It was our club. You'd walk in and see oversize images of the musicians printed on the walls. And it would be full every night. At that time there wasn't much rock and roll yet, there wasn't much electronic music yet. The whole music industry wasn't nearly as powerful, so I guess that's why jazz played a major role in people's lives—to go out and hear live music."

Karl came to New York with Don Cherry's band (Gato Barbieri, Aldo Romano, Jenny Clark, Don, and Karl) in 1966, where they continued to thrive (creatively if not financially). They had worked constantly in the New York clubs. There was also steady work to be had in the public schools, of all places.

"There was a school program that I played in called Young Audiences," says Karl. "Actually, this is where the idea for CMS came

---

1. Ingrid has, at different points in her career, gone under the names Ing Rid, Ingrid Berger, and now Ingrid Sertso.

from. And [we had] an interesting band. I was playing piano. There was Reggie Workman on bass, Horacee Arnold on drums, and Sam Rivers [saxophones] occasionally, Mike Lawrence the trumpet player, sometimes other soloists. So, it was a very hot kind of jazz thing. But it was happening at nine-thirty in the morning! We had to be at the school at nine-thirty, and then do another concert at eleven-thirty at another school, and sometimes at one-thirty at yet another school. Each one would be about forty-five minutes.

"We'd play a tune, and then we'd say, 'This is improvised; so what does it mean to improvise?' And then we'd go through a whole process and finally have one of the kids come up and give us a melody and [we'd] improvise from it; show them how that happens.

"It was a nice little package program, and I did that for years—four years or something like that. I was living in Weehawken, New Jersey, and the program was in all of greater New York City schools . . . and then New Jersey, as well. We also went to Massachusetts at one point. . . . It was a state-funded program; so as long as there weren't any Christmas vacations, we were making money."

At about the same time, Karl got word that John Cage, who had been teaching at New York's New School for Social Research for fifteen years or more, was vacating his position there. Karl conceived a course in improvisation, proposed it in a letter to officials at the New School, and it was accepted. Although John Cage had been teaching his concepts of "chance" relationships in music, which are in many ways akin to improvisation, he was coming at it from a strictly classical background, despite his iconoclasm. Karl, on the other hand, was bringing a jazz musician's sensibilities to the position. "When I went to the first class," Karl recalls, "I remember saying to myself: Don't think about what's going to happen. This is a class about improvisation, and you have to be improvising."

Larry Chernicoff was a member of that class. If one considers that CMS actually began here (and it is plausible to do so), then Larry, who plays vibraphone, guitar, and piano, must be considered the original CMS student. Larry ended up becoming friendly with Karl, Ingrid, and their two young daughters, Eva and Savia, while he was at the New School. Larry remembers that "Karl was living in Weehawken, New Jersey, and I was spending every weekend out there helping him to renovate a garage or something that he was using as a music studio. What ended up happening shortly after that was they went on tour in Europe and asked me if I'd like to come with them. And I did—as a sort of a driver, companion, roadie, and occasional guest member of the band—and spent quite a bit of time in Europe with them. His group at the time was Peter Kowald, the German bass player, and a rather unbelievable drummer by the name of Allen Blairman [and Ingrid, vocals and percussion].[2] I met, through Karl, over there in Europe, Don Cherry, Jan Garbarek, who was an up-and-coming young Scandinavian saxophonist, Steve Lacy . . . just millions of people. It was a really wonderful experience."

Soon, back in New York, Karl began having meetings with Ornette Coleman and others to discuss the formation of the Creative Music Foundation. "Ornette was . . . always the only guy in all of New York supporting what I was doing. He was totally supportive at all times. Everybody else was for protecting their territories or whatever people do. And so Ornette said, 'Yeah, I'll be your cofounder.' He also explained to me that it wasn't really his thing, the nonprofit thing. He wanted to really do it the business way. So, he was cofounding it because he liked the idea, but it wasn't really his beer. He also never taught there. I once asked him, 'Why didn't you ever come up to teach?' And he said, 'Well, you know, then people would think I know something'! That's a typical Ornette Coleman answer. This guy is really unbelievable. If it wasn't for him, I wouldn't have done any of this. He was the one who told me, 'You're absolutely right; go ahead and do it. Don't even wait. Do it now.'"

And so he did. "The actual organization [Creative Music Foundation] was founded in 1971. . . . Ornette sent me to John Cage and Gil Evans and Gunther Schuller. We talked to [Willem] de Kooning, Buckminster Fuller—all these people—and said this is what we want to do."

---

2. This group recorded the album "We Are You" during this tour, on the German Calig label (CAL 30607).

Ornette Coleman

John Cage, New York City, 1973.

2

Escape from New York

*"What's not to like [about CMS]? Basically it was a very honest project.
It was trying to do something creative. It was trying to involve a very
broad spectrum of cultures and ideas, and it was a very inclusive thing.
What's not to like? That's what you're looking for as an artist—to be
involved in things like that."*

—Dave Holland

It wasn't until 1973 that CMS had a home of its own. In the earliest
days, workshops were held in a variety of locations in New York City,
Germany, Italy, Austria, and Woodstock. Karl knew, though, that the
metropolitan New York area was not the place for the Studio as he
envisioned it. It was also not the place to bring up Eva and Savia, then
four and six years old. Marion Brown, the saxophone player, introduced him to Woodstock. "Marion Brown brought me up here," says
Karl. "He's also one of those mystical fellows, who, when they appear,
something is in the works. . . . He introduced me to a few people up
here. This was pretty much the only country place that I knew around
New York. And also, I knew that . . . Dave Holland [the bassist] was
already living here. He was the first one [of those connected with CMS]
to move up here. He was one of my buddies in starting CMS. He was a
teacher from the beginning in the Creative Music Studio. He was
always there, at least once a semester—a great teacher.

"So we decided to come up here and try our luck. I had $700 in
my pocket and two kids in the car, no job, nothing. I did have one part-
time job, actually, at the New School, before I left; and they told me I
could continue that course. I arrived here and went down there, and
the course was cancelled; not enough people signed up. So the only
$500 for the three-month period that I knew was coming in didn't come

in.

"But I had a tape recorder with me—a big professional one. So, I called a radio station in Germany and told them that I will make programs for them. So for the next few months I did radio programs. I put together tapes and whole programs, which they played over there. . . . I just put together tapes, partly from tapes people gave me, partly from tapes I had, and also from records, whatever. It didn't cost me anything, just for the material. So this was the way to survive for the first few months. And then I started to teach, and that was growing very fast. So, basically, in the fall of '72, we already gave workshops here. And we didn't call it Creative Music Studio, yet. . . . The official beginning was in fall of '73."

Ilene Marder, flutist, goes back with Karl and Ingrid to their earliest days in Woodstock. Her recollections are those of a student, but also those of one who came to be involved with the Studio in nearly every way possible. "I became Karl's administrative assistant, I guess you could say. I wrote checks; I did the books, I learned how to do the bookkeeping; I booked the groups; I wrote the grants; I made sure the artists got there; I collected the money; I swept the floors; I played in the band."

Ilene's memory of her first exposure to the music of Karl Berger is tied to a very painful experience: "I can remember being in this apartment on July fourth, 1972. . . . [It was] my first day in Woodstock and I was going to clean, and I wanted some music, so I was putting on all these different borrowed records. And then I came to Karl's and said, hmmm, this looks interesting. So I put it on and said, Hey, this is great cleaning music! So I proceeded to clean the apartment. . . . I opened up the bathroom cabinet, and I started cleaning in an up and down motion. It was an old-fashioned one with a razor stuck in back; and I slit the top of my finger off. This was the Fourth of July. . . . I've always associated hearing Karl for the first time with that moment of . . . spilling blood, you might say."

Soon after that: "I walked into Mowers Market one day and there was this index card: 'Karl Berger, music lessons.' I said, Look at this. I was the first one that called. And they [Karl and family] had just moved here. . . . I happened to have a piano where I lived. So when Karl heard that I had a piano—we had the first class there. He gathered some people about him, and he held the first class at 19 Meadow Court in Bearsville Flats. There were a lot of people who were immediately interested. Karl always had a positive vibe. You had to love what you did with him, because he could make music out of anything—out of the air.

Howie Greenberg

Dave Holland, Woodstock, New York, about 1973.

Ilene Marder, Woodstock, New York, 1973.

"Two or three sessions went by [the very first Creative Music Studio classes], and at some point Karl asked if I had a typewriter. He was trying to write a grant, so he asked me to help him. He needed an assistant, basically. It was never in . . . terms [of being a job]; I was just glad to help.

"What really solidified things was when Karl and Ingrid and the kids moved into Witchtree Road—26A Witchtree Road. It was a beautiful, big, old, converted barn. It was a huge, cavernous space in which Ingrid and Karl put a red carpet. And there was music in that barn! . . . I can remember some fabulous jam sessions—Jack DeJohnette, Dave Holland, people who were generally around at that time [living in or near Woodstock], Stu Martin."

Author Peter Occhiogrosso also has memories of the music that was made in the barn on Witchtree Road. At the time (early seventies), he was perhaps as informed as a journalist could be about the creative music scene in New York—the loft scene, the club scene, the whole avant-garde gamut, and mainstream jazz, too. But Karl's music and the music of CMS stands out with a special clarity for him. "All those characters were around: Jack DeJohnette, Sam Rivers, Lee Konitz, Dave Holland—people who I had seen in the city. That's when I was really just starting my career as a writer, and Karl suggested that I come up and check out the Studio. I took the bus up from New York, and I remember getting off at Witchtree Road at the corner of Route 375, and walking down the road to the Studio, which turned out to be this big, converted barn. I was unpacking my things and just sitting there when Don Cherry, Ed Blackwell, and Karl came in. There were some gamelan [instruments] that had turned up, and the three of them just started an impromptu jam session. I remember being totally entranced by that. I was a casual observer, unpacking my bags, and hearing this music being created on the spur of the moment. Just three guys, who, of course, were each masters in their own right, just sitting down and trying out these new instruments. And the music just flowed out of them so naturally and so organically, so lyrically. It was going on for half an hour or an hour, and I thought, this *really* is the *Creative* Music Studio. The music was just being created on the spot; and, you know, you might never hear something like that in a concert hall or on a record. But it was beautiful, and it really gave me a sense of what Karl was about. That studio was really a place to learn, like an academy of sorts, a jazz academy. I wouldn't even call it jazz. I guess what they were playing would now be called world music—that level of universality.

"I also remember Karl giving lessons and beating out rhythms on his chest—all that kind of stuff that he did, which was a revelation to me. I thought that jazz could be taught two ways. You could go to some place like Berklee [College of Music in Boston] and study with a jazz master there or an academic jazz teacher, or you hung out with someone and carried his bags and learned that way. I didn't think that there was a place where you could be taught universal musical principles the way that Karl and Don [Cherry] and Ed Blackwell and [Anthony] Braxton and DeJohnette and all those people were doing it."

Ingrid

The barn was the birthplace of the CMS magic. This humble building, home to the Bergers and some of the earliest CMS workshops, was resplendent with the creative spirit. The furnishings were sparse—there was no money for niceties. Yet, the simple decorations, the sounds, the lighting, gave the barn an aura that suggested beautiful things would always be welcome there. This was Ingrid's doing. It was in the barn where she began to utilize her special alchemy, with which she would create the mood, the atmosphere, the feeling that let students know: You'll not find another place like this to study music and explore your own creativity—anywhere. It only began in the barn, though. Ingrid created a magical atmosphere wherever CMS took up residence.

Ilene, who lived with Karl and Ingrid in the barn for two years, recalls Christmas there: "Ingrid always gave the place a wonderful eccentricity. The house always felt like that. During Christmas, for example—there were always students, year-round—they put up a Christmas tree for the kids. And they did it in a very German way. . . . You'd walk into this barn, a three-storey barn, with this bright, red carpet, no furniture, Mexican candle lamps that made patterns on the walls all around you, a huge, stone fireplace, and a huge Christmas tree with candles, 'cause that's how they did it in Germany. Everyone just sat there with a sense of wonder and amazement. That personifies, for me, what Ingrid gave to the Studio, and not only on Christmas but at other times."

Karl and Ingrid's opening of their home for workshops and other less formal gatherings was convincing evidence of their commitment to a vision of a creative, musical community. In the beginning, there was actually no separation between CMS and their home and family life. All who came to study music were made to feel as though they were part of the family, and the family was always a part of CMS. Daughters Eva and Savia would involve themselves with creative play during workshops (Ilene remembers them putting on puppet shows to go along with the music), and their mother was always available for them. It was not unusual for Ingrid to have prepared a meal of healthful, vegetarian fare for the participants before or after a workshop. She always has been oriented toward a natural lifestyle, and this carried over into how she nurtured her family and the students.

It seems an extraordinary sacrifice, really, for a woman to open up her home to so much potential disruption. Yet, having a house full of musicians suited Ingrid. "I was raised like that. . . very communal," she says. "I always wanted to be in an artistic environment, because I grew up like that. My mother is a classical piano player, and my older brother is a fantastic painter, and my younger brother is a drummer. . . . It was quite a cool family. . . . Other families talk mainly about money, ours talked mainly about art and music. . . . It was fine that we had the [CMS] workshops in our house. By the time we went to sleep, the workshops were over. That was no problem. Also, I wanted my two daughters to grow up in an artistic community."

Ingrid's own art has many facets. She went through formal vocal training in Europe, but "they were always trying to turn me into an opera singer," she says. She had then and has now a unique singing style. Even though she claims influences as diverse as Billy Holiday and Jimi Hendrix, she has never tried to sound like anyone but herself. Ornette Coleman has said, "Ingrid's voice carries information that translates into all languages, without the need for a translator."

In order to learn more about breathing, expression, and presentation, Ingrid studied acting, both in Germany and at the Marcel Marceau school in Paris. She was looking, though, for training that "worked with the voice the way it is, the natural voice." It wasn't until she came to New York and began studying Indian music with Pandit Pran Nath and his student Lamonte Young that she found it. Indian music opened the door to a new approach to vocal expression that was much more in line with the world-music direction that she and Karl were heading in.

Ingrid has used poetry and text in musical pieces in a way that stretches the conventional connotation of the word *song*. She often writes her own words for pieces or borrows from poetry or prose text. Her way of improvising with words brings drama to a piece, whether or not the piece has a predetermined melody for them to fit into.

Although my interview with Don Cherry for this book was quite brief, one of the strongest points he made was that Ingrid played a role that should not be understated, even though she often seemed to be in the background. "Ingrid was a very important person at CMS," he told me.

Hers was not an up-front, dynamic, role. She was not involved in the business or administration of day-to-day operations. She was, however, always attending to the details of what CMS would look like, how the spaces would be decorated, what the atmosphere would be. Her serenity, her spirituality, and her loving nature suffused the Studio and added considerably to its character. "She's a true artist," says Ilene. "There ain't no one like her."

Karl Berger in the barn, 1973.

Raymond Ross

Ed Blackwell, New York City, 1974.

3

Music Universe, Music Mind

"If you can talk you can sing. If you can walk you can dance."
—African proverb

To understand how the Creative Music Studio experience expanded musicians' self expression, it is necessary to think in terms of the elements of music and to acknowledge the similarities among all musical traditions rather than the differences. The differences are mere details; they are not what makes music music. Many people ask what "kind" of music was played at CMS? It's natural for them to wonder. And it's commonly assumed that CMS was a place to learn jazz. The opportunity to learn jazz was there, unquestionably. But CMS was, above all, a place to learn music. It just happened that most of the musicians whom Karl Berger was associated with and who could work and teach music as a personal expression in a universal context were labeled jazz musicians.

I learned from Karl Berger and the Creative Music Studio experience that all music reaches us and colors our experience through its elements of rhythm, melody, and harmony. This is true regardless of the style of the music, the historic period of the music, or the skill level of the musicians who bring the music to us. All musicians work to develop the ability to play in time and in tune. The raw materials of music are universal. Yet, the perception or expression of them often help us to portray our uniqueness as individuals.

Music is as inextricable from the human experience as is the sexual urge. We are all musical beings. Musical expression actually predates any of our known musical instruments. There has always been the human body and there has always been the voice. And from the beginning of time there have been, external to the human body, materials for the drum or rhythm instrument—rocks and sticks, if nothing else. Every cultural or ethnic group throughout human history has had some form of music to express their humanity. Some of us believe that only certain, special individuals have the capacity to express themselves through music. This is not true. This is only a belief that is imposed through socialization. Someone makes fun of a child when she sings; she is stung by the experience and therefore represses her urge to sing. Another child loves the rhythm and is moved to dance, but is admonished to quit "acting up." An adolescent may feel compelled to pursue a career in music. However, his parents assure him that if he does, he'll be on the road to failure and poverty. They work to convince him that he doesn't have what those who succeed in music have.

There is no such thing as a person without innate musical capabilities. If you can perceive time and space, you can express yourself musically. Some choose to develop the music within themselves. And this, too, is oftentimes a factor of socialization. We play music because our parents played music. Or, we play music because those whom we respect the most played music. In American society, it is far more acceptable for black people to play music of self expression than it is for white people.

Karl has developed a system of conveying the universal quality of odd and even that typifies all musical structures. Odd and even elements characterize linear, rhythmic relationships and vertical, polyrhythmic relationships. Karl represents this odd-and-even universality with the syllables *ga ma la ta ki*. Gamala represents three, or an odd grouping. Taki represents two, or an even grouping. Armed with an understanding of gamala taki, a musician can reduce any seemingly complex rhythmic cycle to groups of two and three. A pattern of seven (7/4 or 7/8 time) is merely two groups of two and a group of three. Whether you count taki taki gamala, taki gamala taki, or gamala taki taki depends on the phrasing of the melody.

A cycle of twenty-two is no more complex. It consists of two groups of eleven, each of which consists of three threes and a two. Three is as high as you ever need to count! And there is no music that has ever been played or ever will be played that cannot be characterized by these simple, odd-and-even rhythmic groupings.

Harmony, too, begins with similar, simple mathematical proportions. At a basic level you have fourths and fifths, and it becomes more complex from there. By becoming more highly aware of numeric proportions in rhythm, one can gain a greater sensitivity to the details of harmony. It all begins with rhythm. "The proprtions that you feel harmonically are all vibrational," Karl says. "So that means they are rhythmical. If you have a higher pitch and compare it to a lower pitch, the main difference is that there are more beats to the vibration of that [higher] pitch. So, therefore, you can feel it rhythmically. . . . If you get a real strong feel for rhythm, then your feel for harmony follows quite naturally. . . . The whole world works vibrationally; that means rhythmically. . . . I noticed that when people did the gamala taki [rhythm training] for four to six weeks, that they would be tuning better, that their sound would improve. And not because they practiced the sound, but because they practiced the rhythms. That's why rhythm training is so basic to all music training."

I asked Karl about the origin of gamala taki. He told me, "When I started playing with Don Cherry, in his band in Paris, he came one night with a tune, and he said, 'We're gonna play this tune. It's called "Gamala Gamala Taki."'" And Don Cherry was the kind of guy who . . . would listen to short-wave radio all the time, or whatever. Anything that he would hear he would instantly transform and use in his music. Ornette once called him 'the man with the elephant memory.' He has the kind of memory that if he hears one thing, he can reproduce it.

"I said what is that ["Gamala Gamala Taki"]? And he played some melody in three, three, two. He said, 'You just count it like three, three, two, but you don't use the numbers; use the syllables.' Obviously, he had heard that on a radio. But he later never knew where that came from. It could have been anywhere. It sounds to me like Middle Eastern, Afghanistan, wherever. A few weeks later, it struck me that all melodies could be constructed in that way, in an additive manner. So, that's how it came about."

Basic gamala taki practice is conducted in a group. At a typical CMS session, the group might include everyone enrolled plus some interested local folks from Woodstock. (Or it might be only four or five people. Not everyone saw a benefit in this type of training.) One need not be a musician to take part.

The group sits in a circle. Everyone begins to pat his or her legs with open palms, alternating left, right, (or right, left—It doesn't matter) in a steady tempo set by the leader. The object is to synchronize the group's time keeping and maintain a meditative state of mind. At the same time, the group begins a chant of the syllables gamala taki, arranged in whatever cycle the leader has established. It could be a group of seven syllables, or it could be made more complex by repeating a cycle of three groups of seven, each group in a different sequence.

Even cycles (six, eight, twelve, etc.) are more natural and easy to feel. Working with and overcoming the challenge of odd cycles gives an even greater feeling of looseness and freedom with the rhythm. By imposing a chant of odd-numbered syllables over an even beat (having only two hands and alternating right, left, right, left means that the pattern must remain even), the dominance of the rhythmic feel constantly shifts from one side of the body to the other. The body forgets that there is any awkwardness in playing odd time signatures. After enough practice, one can play—and solo—as naturally in odd time as in even.

After the group settles into the rhythm, Karl might begin to substitute notes of an improvised melody for the syllables *gamala taki*. Everyone eventually joins in, and the group is now singing a melody on top of the rhythmic cycle. Ingrid now may introduce a melodic pattern that works against the given accents. Harmonies emerge. The intensity increases. Soon an entire spontaneous composition takes form, which is often a moving piece of music. The more a participant focuses on the timing and the tuning, listening and remaining mindful in the moment, the more this training will enhance his or her musicality.

The method and idea of gamla taki practice are likely to have a more pervasive influence than Karl ever expected. I contacted Ed Sarath, head of the jazz department at the University of Michigan School of Music, about the possibility of bringing Karl to the University. He was nearly dumbfounded. He had attended a workshop in Banff, Alberta, Canada at the Banff Centre School of Fine Arts (sort of a CMS on the road) in 1981. The experience of basic gamala taki practice had strongly affected him. He began teaching gamala taki at the University of Michigan and had even started writing a book on the practice. However, he had no idea how to contact Karl—until I called him.

Using syllables instead of numbers to represent rhythmic patterns is also typical of Indian and African drumming. I can recall sitting with a group on the lawn of the CMS grounds on a gorgeous, sunny, spring day. Don Cherry was explaining the syllables that Indian tabla players employ in remembering or singing complex and lengthy rhythmic cycles. On another day, we gathered at Karl's home to hear Jumma Santos speak of how African drumming is closely related to the spoken language.

The other side of basic music practice at CMS dealt with pitch and involved training the mind and the ear to be more in tune. It was typically Ingrid who directed this portion of the sessions. She had a way of simplifying some of Karl's concepts of basic musical practice that brought them down to Earth. She developed a method of hearing and tuning that utilized the voice, yet was for all instrumentalists, as was

*Karl Berger
with student
group in the
barn, 1973.*

Ingrid Sertso, Woodstock, New York, 1973.

the rhythm training.

Through her training in Indian music, Ingrid discovered that the srudi box, also called a *swar-peti*, was a very effective tool for training the ear and the voice. The srudi box is a drone instrument, which Indian performers use to provide a constant, droning, tonal reference point. It is something like a bellows that forces air across reeds, making a sound similar to a harmonica or an accordian. The tonic note and complex series of overtones that the instrument creates provide a broad range of pitches to which a musician may match the voice or an instrument. Ingrid regards it as a grounding, spiritual, supportive instrument. "You have the Earth for a support," she says. "The drone is actually the sound for the Earth."

Basic tuning practice was very similar to the basic rhythm practice: All participants would gather in a circle, and someone, usually Ingrid but not always, would play the srudi box. Everyone was to simultaneously find a pitch within the overtones and match it with a vocal tone in a comfortable range. It was a breathing exercise, a meditation exercise, a listening exercise, and an exercise in continuous adjustment of one's pitch to the reference pitch. If the first tone became uncomfortable, one could find another pitch to tune to. In this way, everyone could experience what it is like to be tune and to maintain their tuning over time, changing the pitch if need be, but always remaining focused. All members of the group were free to sing higher or lower, louder or softer, as they pleased, as long as they were in tune with the srudi box. The entire group could, in this way, produce a beautifully tuned, constantly shifting chorus, without anyone having to know a melody or chord changes.

Then it would get scary. The group would bring the sound level down so that each member, one at a time, could sing on top of the sound of the whole. We were encouraged, as soloists (even though very few real singers ever participated), to improvise freely, always staying in tune with the srudi box.

It was intimidating to open our mouths and sing. In fact, some people would simply refuse to expose themselves in that way. "The voice is the first thing that gets repressed in your childhood," according to Ingrid. "So people are very shy about singing." She has also said that "the voice is the strongest manifestation of your personality."

It followed, then, that those who were willing to make themselves uncomfortable and sing benefitted by improving their tuning, but also by improving their sense of self as performers.

There is no way that we can speak of universal elements of

music and not address the concept of improvisation. It may seem odd to some American and European music makers and listeners, but most musical forms of the world are not notated. Written music is predominantly a Western method of perpetuating musical traditions. The rest of the world relies on oral and improvisatory traditions to communicate among musicians.

It was inevitable, though, that improvisational forms assert themselves as traditions in Western music. This began in America with the music that has been called *jazz*. I say that it was inevitable because improvisational music is the only way that the human spirit, which will not be repressed, can be fully expressed through sound.

Jazz (and the improvisational musical styles that have grown out of it but are not truly suited to that label because of their distance from the culture that spawned jazz) is the music of the individual. European classical music, despite having been the product of some of the most creative minds in our history, is dependent upon the individual musician's ability to adhere technically to a written composition.

The classical musician's role is not to create, but to replicate the sounds represented by notes on a page and not alter the collective rendering of the composition. Individual freedom of expression in classical music is antithetical to the spirit of the performance of these pieces, which required the highest level of creativity of only the composer. This is not intended in any way, however, to disparage European classical music. It is simply to make the distinction between musical forms that require an individual musician to express himself freely—in essence, to compose as he goes—and music that requires that an individual be technically proficient in reproducing the sounds that the composer intended and in blending those sounds with the collective.

"The music doesn't come from the instrument. It comes from the mind behind it."

—Leo Smith

The goal at CMS was to allow individual musicians the freedom to develop their own innate musicality, to work with the elements of music, and to create methods that would allow them to discover their own sounds. This discovery teaches that the tools of creative expression lie within; they are not to be assembled from the external environment. It is a process of unveiling what already exists. Musicians at CMS were encouraged to go beyond traditions and styles and work with what was common to all musics. This was what made it so natural for people from Senegal, Canada, Finland, or New Jersey to get together and create a sound that was uniquely theirs and undeniably valid.

We seek to master the universal elements of music by paying ever closer attention to their details. By empowering our "music minds" we come to a more complete understanding of what it really means to play in tune and in time.

Karl explains: "The mind training that I was doing with the students by way of the gamala taki and rhythmic training was very much along the lines of the mind training in Zen Buddhism, for example. What I call the music mind was what was being practiced in Zen. That was not something that I noticed first; I think John Cage noticed that first—the connection of the mind state of music making, or any artistic endeavor, with the mind state of the meditator. Like, not to think as you do it, or not to think about what you do as you do it. Because, when you think, it's either too early or too late. So you're missing the point. You have to learn to be at that note that you're just about to play without putting your mind right on top of it, which is the big mistake that most people make. That's why the music gets too heavy or too nervous."

Karl manifests the music universe concept in his construction of large orchestral ensembles. These have, at various times, been called the CMS Orchestra, the Woodstock Workshop Orchestra, or the Music Universe Orchestra. Membership has typically comprised a combination of CMS students and guiding artists.

As Karl explained in a CMS promotional publication (about 1980):

> "The Music Universe Orchestra combines the core elements of a classical chamber ensemble (strings, woodwinds) with those of a jazz ensemble (horns, rhythm group) and world-music soloists in all sections (percussion, melody). Very unusual and exciting collaborations (duets, trios, etc) as well as standard combinations (string quartet, woodwind quartet, jazz combo) emerge from the changing colors of the orchestral sound. Formats and interpretations of shifting stylistic dominance develop. Actual traditional materials are being introduced that way.
>
> Although the elements of a performance are carefully prepared in rehearsals, it is my experience that each concert is a unique experience. Music Universe can happen with any group of proficient musicians anywhere in the world."

The unique experience of a performance by the Music Universe Orchestra owes not only to the all encompassing instrumental groupings, but also to the compositions themselves. Karl goes on to say:

"The particular compositional processes that I use are not all new. Rhythmic and melodic-harmonic elements (beats, intervals) are used in systematic number combinations not unlike certain forms of periodic compositions or jazz compositions or the number applications that, for example, Bach, Bartok, or Messiaen used. Of course, the results are very different and, I hope, recognizable for their individual touch.

One of the main differences is the open- endedness of the created parts: The actual written parts are subject to interpretation in their actual sound and in their melodic and rhythmic development. They become modular elements in the total composition, which emphasizes the highly sophisticated improvisatory skills that all world-music players of stature command.

To my mind, the key to successful world-music communication is the balance of preconceived and improvised elements. . . . In this context of a world-music orchestra, the composer becomes the conducting organizer of the total sound potential provided by the written parts and oral/improvisatory resources.

I am fascinated with the idea of simple, very basic decisions shaping the compositional modules. Various grades of complexity develop naturally through their collective and contrapuntal use. I am equally fascinated with the potential for interpretation and improvisation that each musician consciously or unconsciously has in store, a resource that is rarely used to any substantial extent."

4

Why Woodstock?

"I hated to see it [CMS] go . . . because I haven't seen anyone take such a wide approach to the music. . . . It not only affected me, but my whole family as well. I can remember taking my whole family there and just hanging out."

—Oliver Lake

You must understand the power of the place. Woodstock is magnetic; it draws creative, spiritual people from all over the globe and has done so since the early nineteenth century. The physical beauty of Woodstock and the surrounding Catskills is undeniable. The mountains are not dramatic or majestic like the Rockies or the Alps. The steep, rocky, rough, wooded hillsides have a subtle aura of enchantment. Everywhere there are streams, brooks, and rivulets of varying sizes. Sloping meadows and the flat plain of the Hudson Valley to the east make it an area of contrast. There's some sort of magic there.

It's hard to believe, when you're in the midst of that serene environment, that the noise, dirt, and density of New York City are only a couple hours away. It is this juxtaposition, though, that gives Woodstock its distinctiveness. Along with the grime and crime of New York City, you have one of the planet's strongest concentrations of artists, writers, and musicians. As long as there has been an arts scene and a Greenwich Village in New York City, there have been creative souls who have sought rural refuge in Woodstock. Babatunde Olatunji, African drummer and cultural educator, recalls his many trips from New York to Woodstock. "Even before you get to CMS, you know that your whole attitude is changing. Coming from a city like New York, a concrete jungle, you pass through woodlands, you hear birds singing— it's country. You become aware of all of the things that nature has given to us to admire that we seldom take a look at. So, going there was usually therapeutic for many people."

Woodstock's Arts Tradition

Ralph Radcliffe Whitehead, a wealthy Briton, established the first arts colony in Woodstock in 1902. Alf Evers, in his book *Woodstock: History of an American Town* talks of the movement and the writers that gave Whitehead his impetus:

> "The arts and crafts movement, by 1902 several genera-
> tions old, had begun as an act of protest against some of
> the evil effects of the Industrial Revolution. The big
> thinkers of the movement, men like Thomas Carlyle,
> John Ruskin, and William Morris, pointed out that work-
> ers were deprived of the wholesome satisfaction of car-
> rying the making of products from beginning to end when
> objects were made in factories by the use of steam or
> water power and with a division of labor in effect. These
> workers were no more than machine tenders laboring
> for wages rather than for the joy of creative effort. The
> crowding of workers into factory slums and the heart-
> less organization of child labor for industrial profit might
> be swept away if only men might return to the old sys-
> tem of handicrafts."[1]

Whitehead was influenced also by the art colonies that were becoming common in Europe at the time. These were, however, more or less spontaneous developments that arose from artists' tendencies to gather in places where nature offered bounties of landscapes to paint. Byrdcliffe, as Whitehead's colony came to be called, was, however, a well thought out, carefully planned, self-sustaining community.

While reading Evers' book, I was struck by the similarities be-
tween the founding of both Byrdcliffe and the Creative Music Studio. Both were attempts to set up creative communities, in spite of the prevailing commercialism that was antithetical to their cause and the lack of economic support from the social structure. Both relied on the tranquility and serenity of the area's physical beauty for artistic stimulus. They also depended on their proximity to New York City as a wealth of

---

1. Alf Evers, *Woodstock: History of an American Town* (Woodstock: Overlook, 1987), 403.

creative input, in people and ideas and as a link to the rest of the world.

CMS and Byrdcliffe were driven by the idealism of individuals of European descent. Karl Berger, a German, and Ralph Whitehead, an Englishman, each possessed the type of creative determination that would bring their respective communities into being, regardless of the obstacles. They differ, however, in one significant area. Whitehead had the benefit of his family's fortune, made in textiles, with which to start Byrdcliffe. He bought up several farms and was able to build dwellings and studios according to his own vision. Karl, on the other hand, started from scratch. He used credit cards to finance the rental of his first properties. I can't help but believe that if CMS had the financial backing that Byrdcliffe had, it would be operating today.

Byrdcliffe drew artists from all over. Some, disenchanted with Whitehead's way of doing things, split off to found their own artistic communities. Most notable of these was Hervey White, who created a colony called Maverick. To finance Maverick, White staged festivals in the 1920s that were in many ways the precursors of the celebrated Woodstock Music and Art Fair of 1969. These were colorful, bawdy affairs, with theater, music, dancing, arts and crafts, costumed revellers, and huge crowds. They helped to more firmly entrench an antiartists sentiment that has been a source of animosity in the community and which still lingers in the wake of Woodstock '94, the twenty-fifth anniversary of the 1969 festival.

Aquarian Age

It has been, however, the artists and their colonies that have given the little town its reputation, which continues to attract leading visual artists, writers, musicians, and other performing artists from around the world. In the 1960s, as mass marketing and recording technology began to spawn the enormous music industry that has come to be, musicians began to play a much larger role in shaping Woodstock's artistic landscape. And, of course, there was the counter-culture aura— the whole hippie thing. In 1970, the first issue of the Woodstock *Aquarian* had this to say: "Welcome to Woodstock and the Aquarian Age . . . Woodstock a town, but more a name that symbolizes a state of consciousness . . . this valley rumored by the Indians who lived here many moons ago to to be haunted with strange spirits, a sacred kind of place . . . Woodstock a Mecca for the culture of the new age . . . Poet-prophet Bob Dylan brought attention to this area when he first came. The pop heroes who either live, or have lived here are many. The Band,

Tim Hardin, Paul Butterfield, Jimmy [sic] Hendrix . . .ˮ[2]

Albert Grossman, perhaps the most successful rock and folk impresario and manager, set up a residence and recording studio in neighboring Bearsville. John Sebastian of The Lovin' Spoonful, folk artists Happy and Artie Traum, and rock star Todd Rundgren, also became fixtures on the Woodstock scene.

Jazz artists began to take up residence in the area in the late sixties. These were folks who had already established themselves in New York and around the world and preferred the peacefulness of the Catskills: Dave Holland, Jack DeJohnette, Anthony Braxton, Howard Johnson, Carla Bley, and others. In the seventies, Karl Berger and his wife Ingrid came to town, as did a legion of musicians whose initial contact with Woodstock was through the Creative Music Studio.

Being in close proximity to neighbors such as these gave CMS students who took up residence in Woodstock opportunities for some unique interactions. Saxophonist Donnie Davis talks of his neighbor, Anthony Braxton: "He was my main man up there for a while. I really love Anthony. I lived in a cabin for $55 a month within earshot of Anthony's house; so we were neighbors for several years. We became friends and stuff. I didn't really study with him all that much, actually. I just took some lessons with him.... I used to be intimidated because I'd be practicing in my little $55-a-month cabin, by the stream, with an outhouse. And he'd be walking right by—he was always walking down the street, smoking his pipe. I'd have to, like, suddenly stop. He used to give me some shit sometimes. He'd say, 'Davis you're sounding too good on flute, there. You'd better stop it. I'm gonna come over and throw a cream pie in your face.' . . . I once asked him how he did that triple-tonguing. I said, 'Anthony, that's incredible. How do you tongue so fast?' He said, 'Don, there's a rubber band in my mouth—and it's called paranoia.'ˮ

A Spirit Place

Spiritual seekers have also found Woodstock to be a very hospitable place. Perhaps it's the natural beauty; perhaps it's something more. The native settlers who first made the Hudson Valley their home left behind numerous tales of the spiritual power that was rife in the hills, caves, trees, rivers, and the very air of the Catskills. Alf Evers' book

---

2. Alf Evers, *Woodstock: History of an American Town* (Woodstock: Overlook, 1987), 668.

Don Cherry taking flight with Eagle Eye Cherry, Sarah Carey, Eva Berger, Savia Berger, Woodstock, New York, late 1970s.

Woodstock Workshop Orchestra in performance, 1979.

has an entire section devoted to the magic, conjuring, and witchcraft that the area inspired in the 1800s. One of the early homes of the Creative Music Studio was a converted Lutheran camp (which many have called a monastery, but there's no evidence to suggest that monks ever resided there) in nearby Mt. Tremper. This imposing stone edifice and its pastoral grounds are now home to the Zen Meditation Center. Another place, which the CreativeMusic Foundation nearly bought, ended up being a monastery for Tibetan Buddhists. It was an old boarding house on Mead's Mountain, which boasts a commanding view of the town of Woodstock and the surrounding area. Karl's tale of how the property ultimately went to the Tibetans has, itself, something of a mystic air:

"This old lama, Kalu Rinpoche. . . drove by the [Mead] house and pointed to it and said 'This is the Dharma Center.' When I heard that I asked him what he meant by that, and he didn't know. He said, 'Did I say that?' And he was sort of twinkling with his eyes. I know from my experience with the Tibetans, which goes back to '74 or something, that they never say anything they don't mean. So I knew that it was not the place for us. I told the owner, who was a real neurotic, former air force pilot, who lived there just 'cause it looked like the final approach, and who would never let anyone come in; he was very paranoid and still wanted to sell the place. I told him we are not buying the place, the Tibetans will buy it.[3]

"He just looked at me and said, 'Where'd you get that from?' I said 'Well, this lama said that, and they never say anything they don't mean.' And he thought I was crazy, because we had a deal, you know. We [CMF] were getting ready to do this [buy the place]. I said, 'Listen, I'm not going to do this, the Tibetans are going to do this.

"About three or four months went by and nothing happened. One day he called me, this guy—Captain Milo was his name—he called me at CMS and said, 'You were wrong. I'm selling this house to this hotelier. He's coming up this afternoon to sign the papers.' I called him in the evening and said, 'Did you sign the papers?' And he said, 'Come up!' So I went up and the guy was totally out of it, because an hour before this contract was supposed to be signed, the Tibetans came and gave him the money. They came in . . . and they had a check, $200,000

---

3. The Mead's Mountain property became the Karma Triyana Dharma-chakra, one of a handful of major Tibetan Buddhist centers in the United States and the American seat of the Karmapa. In 1992 a new monastery was built adjacent to the original Mead's Mountain House, which still stands.

or whatever it was. They gave it to him and said they'd come back in four weeks.

"It's interesting, isn't it? They told Milo that he could stay as longas he wanted; they would give him some rooms. 'Cause he was living there alone in this huge thing. So for two months Milo was sitting in the middle of this [Buddhist activity]. He couldn't believe it. . . . He was a very strange person. He had not made any plans; he just couldn't hold on to the house. Actually, Bob Dylan once wanted to buy it. [Milo] kicked him out because he came barefoot. The guy probably had the money in his back pocket!"

5

The Itinerant CMS

"Artists teach people how to live."
—Lester Bowie

Documentation was not a priority for Karl, Ilene, and the early administration. Consequently, the memories of those involved remain the best reference sources for the events of the first few years. However, after twenty-some years those memories take on a certain wispiness. All concur, though, that the search for a home, a place where workshops, students, and guiding artists could dwell together, took up a good deal of the enterprise's energy at first.

Students who attended the first Witchtree Road sessions were on their own for housing until CMS got it together to rent a boarding house from Woodstocker Joan Schwartzberg. This is where the first, full semester session was held. Ilene recalls taking Karl's long-distance instructions for running the new facility, while Karl taught workshops in Europe. By phone, they coordinated logistics for the boarding-house rental, promoted the Woodstock sessions, admitted students, and whatever else had to be done. They were both beginners in organizing anything on this scale.

The next place that became home-away-from home for CMS students was a place called Ashwood House. Workshops continued to take place at the barn on Witchtree Road and later at the old Lutheran camp in nearby Mt. Tremper. Housing accomodations, though, from about 1973 through 1975 were at the rented Ashwood House. The Creative Music Foundation owned no property until 1977, when it entered a lease-buy arrangement with Oehler's Mountain Lodge.

Ashwood House was the first of a succession of properties (rooming houses, so to speak) that provided a tangential education for

CMS students as experiments in group living. It had a homey atmosphere, but it was entirely up to the students to maintain it. Sleeping rooms were upstairs and the students shared a large kitchen. It was common to come down in the morning and find stretching and movement classes in session (unless, of course, you had gotten up early enough to be a participant in these invaluable sessions).

Stu Martin

Drummer Bob Moses relates an incident from that time that illustrates the idiosyncratic nature of one of CMS's more colorful characters, drummer Stu Martin. A *Woodstock Times* article from January of 1975 reports that Stu had "performed on over fifty albums, playing with the likes of Basie, Ellington, and Quincy Jones."[1] He was also director of music at Washington, D.C.'s International University of Communications.

Bob says that this particular incident stands out in his mind because it was "hilarious, but kind of cruel. . . . One of the people who studied with me," Bob recalls, "was one of the drummers playing in Stu's ensemble. . . . I was watching them play, and it was maybe ten or twelve people—wailin',just full out, free-form chaos. It was a couple of drummers, maybe three keyboards. You know how the instrumentation never really made any particular sense; it was whoever showed up— like, four violin players, two keyboards, maybe two drummers, a bass clarinet, and a couple of acoustic guitars, which you couldn't hear. There had to have been maybe ten or fifteen people, and it was completely just [at this point Bob vocalizes over the phone, quite accurately, what ten or fifteen people playing total chaos might sound like]. I couldn't make out what any one person was playing; it wasn't like there was any separation.

"And I remember, Stu stopped the whole group in the middle and, like, went off on this guy who was playing drums, saying, 'you tasteless motherfucker!' In that context, what would constitute taste? What could the guy have done that was so wrong? What was right and what was wrong? This poor guy was traumatized for weeks trying to figure out what
he had done. I thought that was really funny, even though it was kind of cold. I mean, I don't know what Stu was thinkin'. . . . But that cracked me up— 'you tasteless motherfucker.'"

---

1. "Two Faces of Jazz," *Woodstock Times*, January 2, 1975, p. 10.

Stu's eccentricities found a more positive outlet in the weekly radio show that he developed, called "CMS Presents Everything," which aired on WKNY in Kingston, New York.

"Everything"? Well, it did include a Sunday mystery show. "Mark Stone, Private Investigator," was performed live at the Woodstock Town Hall and featured six actors and a live CMS orchestra, directed by Stu Martin.

The public was invited, and the event was videotaped. The orchestra's role was unique in that it was quite possibly the first time that an orchestra had accompanied a live radio drama with absolutely no written music. "Everything will be improvised on the spot," Stu told the *Woodstock Times,* "The choice and responsibility of what the music sounds like will belong to each musician."[2]

Eva and Savia Berger, Karl's daughters, added to the regular broadcast by reading poetry and telling the riddle of the week. Stu's eighteen-month-old son Ezekial, "the wizard," provided the sound of the week. Tapes of CMS student works were also featured, as were astrology, artist interviews, and public-affairs announcements. "Everyone will be a part of everything," according to Stu. It was not unusual, actually, to hear someone's pet on the air.

Portability

In the fall of 1975, student housing moved to the Lutheran camp at Mt. Tremper, about twelve miles outside of Woodstock. This building and its grounds added considerably to the aura of magic and enchantment that was typical of the Studio. The grand, stone structure had a sort of medieval quality about it. It was, essentially, a large church with dormitory-type rooms, assembly rooms, offices, and a large kitchen.

Some like to tell stories of spirits that inhabited the place. Doors and windows would mysteriously open and close during practice or recording sessions. On calm days winds would whip up inside the building. There were spirits present.

The grounds had an enchanted-forest feeling that was so characteristic of the Catskills and which made it a memorable spot from which to watch the seasons turn the surrounding mountains from winter gray to shimmering greens. Deer would often come down from the wooded hillside that rose away from the property and graze on the immense sloping lawn. Sunny, warm days made practicing outdoors

---

2. "'CMS Presents Everything.'" *Woodstock Times*, February 13, 1975.

irresistible.

In these early times, Karl was establishing what Larry Chernicoff calls a "portable CMS concept." Larry had reunited with Karl after a brief stay at Boston's Berklee College of Music, where he studied with Gary Burton. His intention was to take off one semester from Berklee to check out what Karl was up to in Woodstock. That semester ended up becoming six years, in which Larry studied, taught, and worked for Karl in every capacity that he was skilled for. He even developed new skills as needed. Their association continues to this day.

Larry explains CMS's portability: "We were doing classes in Manhattan a couple of days a week at the Turtle Bay Music School [These 1973 sessions featured Karl Berger, Frederic Rzewski, Bob Moses, Gordon Mumma, John Cage, Lee Konitz, Sam Rivers, Barry Altschul, David Izenson, George Russell, Garrett List, and Musica Elettronica Viva with Richard Teitelbaum]. We were in Woodstock on Mondays, Wednesdays, and Fridays, then Karl and [bassist] Tom Schmidt and I would be down in New York a couple nights a week—driving down and doing basic practice and workshops and playing sessions. . . .

"In all of the time that I was involved in the Studio, it was in Woodstock and New York and Albany; in Canada [Banff Centre School of Fine Arts], in Ohio at Antioch College; workshops in Germany and workshops in the Netherlands; Naropa Institute in Colorado, which was really rather amazing. . . . Karl's energy and his lifestyle. . . [made it] a portable situation; and wherever there were people interested, there was a session and there was often a performance.

"He would go in, and in one day bring his music cycles and rehearse the people—absolutely regardless of what the instrumentation was. . . . You could have eighteen basses, a tuba, and a piccolo—and he'd play a concert for the public that night. It was really a road show. So, in addition to all of the people who came to Woodstock, he touched the lives of musicians all over the world."

In 1972, Karl held the Summer Studio for Musical improvisation in Heidelberg, Germany. In 1973, there was the Creative Music Summer Studio in Rome and the premier of the Music Universe Orchestra at a Berlin Philharmonic TV concert. There was also a lot of CMS activity in New York City during the period from 1973 to 1976, all of which helped get word into the media of what was going on in Woodstock.

In 1974, CMS held a ten-day intensive session of concerts and workshops at Ornette Coleman's Artist House loft in New York. This was a nationally advertised event that was more widely promoted than anything had been up to that point. Larry Chernicoff remembers it as "one of the most successful things that Karl ever put together for the

Larry Chernicoff, Woodstock, New York, 1975.

*Jack DeJohnette and Dave Holland, Artists House, New York City,
1974.*

Studio. [It was an] amazing set of workshops and concerts every night at Ornette Coleman's place, which I'll never forget. . . .

I remember that one of the participants was John Scofield, the guitarist. There was one concert by the Gateway Trio, with Jack DeJohnette, Dave Holland, and John Abercrombie. And something happened that I had never seen up to that point. It was a very, very hot summer night, and Dave Holland put down his acoustic bass and picked up an electric bass, which I had never seen him play. He and Jack DeJohnette then broke into some of the major, classic sections from Miles Davis's 'In a Silent Way,'[3] which was the album that brought both of them to the attention of the public. And Jack DeJohnette [took] a drum solo where he didn't hit anything; it was a pantomime drum solo."

Naropa

The Peace Church Concert series was another memorable New York highlight of 1974. The Music Universe Orchestra (featuring Karl Berger, Ingrid Berger, Ilene Marder, Larry Chernicoff, Frederic Rzewski, Lee Konitz, Sam Rivers, Dan Carter, Garrett List, Dave Holland, David Izenson, Jonathan Kline, Tom Schmidt, Steve Haas, Bob Moses, Gregory Reeve, and Richard Teitelbaum) performed ten concerts in a New York City church in March, April, and May. A live, double album resulted, as did a good deal of publicity.

One piece on the album featured text from the book *Meditation in Action*, a book that had given Ingrid solace in troubled times. It was she who had chosen the words and used them as lyrics for the piece. The author, Chögyam Trungpa Rinpoche, had granted the Bergers permission to use the text, and after hearing the album invited them to teach at his Naropa Institute in Boulder, Colorado, an institute established for the study of the arts and psychology in the context of Tibetan Buddhism. Trungpa thought that Karl's concepts of music as a universal and intrinsic element of humanity would be a natural fit within the curriculum at Naropa, and apparently he was right.

Karl, ever eager to take his "road show" wherever there were people who had an interest, packed up his family and his instruments in his van in the summer of 1975 and made for Colorado. Thus began the Bergers' relationship with Trungpa Rinpoche and Naropa, a connection that would strengthen their interest and involvement in Tibetan Buddhism and affect the evolution of CMS in ways both direct

---

3. Although Larry said "In a Silent Way," I believe that the album he was referring to was "Bitches' Brew."

and indirect.

Tom Schmidt, who also made the trip, told me of the eight-week jaunt with a flair and flavor that evoked Jack Kerouac's *On the Road*. Tom was another of the core group of people who were with Karl from the earliest days and who made the running of CMS a full-time commitment. He had studied bass with Charlie Haden and was a valuable assistant in the basic practice sessions, teaching rhythm and tuning. He described an adventure that took in not only the two weeks at Naropa, but also brought the portable CMS to Antioch College in Ohio, South Bend, Indiana, Cuernavaca, Mexico, San Diego, California, and other stops in between.

There were "beautiful gigs" at colleges and clubs, as Tom recalls. There was also a brush with the border patrol in Texas as they returned to the U.S. after their weeks in Mexico. "I thought they were looking for drugs," says Tom. "We had this big white van with New York plates; they might have thought we were smuggling people in. They said 'where you coming from?' 'Cuernavaca.' 'Where you goin'?' 'San Diego.' I don't know what we looked like to these guys."

Tom had good reason to be nervous, but not because they had been pegged by the border patrol as smugglers. He had no driver's license.

Karl and Ingrid presented CMS-style workshops at Naropa in the summers of 1975 and 1976. They were accompanied on different trips by Ilene Marder and Larry Chernicoff. Dave Holland came out to teach, as did Ed Blackwell, Don Cherry, and Collin Walcott from the group Oregon.

Writers William Burroughs, Allen Ginsberg, and Ed Sanders also taught at Naropa concurrent with the CMS residency. Ginsberg and Sanders, who ran the Jack Kerouac School of Disembodied Poetics at Naropa held poetry workshops at CMS in Woodstock in 1978, the first year in which the Studio incorporated words and poetry into the program.

During their time together at Naropa, Karl accompanied Allen Ginsberg on piano for the first public performance of Ginsberg's song "Father Death Blues." Ginsberg recalls the event with some amusement: "I must say, despite his brilliance as a jazz musician and as a performer, he couldn't get it right. The cadence is not exactly one, two, three, four, or anything like that. It depends on the vocalization. . . . He couldn't get it off the four-square rhythmic rigidity. It was very funny, actually. And I was hesitant to criticize it, because I didn't know anything about music. I thought maybe I was wrong. After all, the thing is based on my own voice. . . . But we got it through, and I think there's a recording of it in the Naropa archives."

The Bergers and Trungpa Rinpoche, who later paid two visits to CMS, remained close until Trungpa's death in 1987. In fact, it was Trungpa Rinpoche who gave Ingrid the name Sertso (meaning "gold lake of understanding"), which she uses as a surname today. Ingrid cites him as one of the "main influences" in her life. And certainly, the spiritual depth that she developed through Tibetan Buddhism has been one of the main influences on the course that she, Karl, and the Studio have taken. What was (and is) so appealing to Karl and Ingrid is that the state of mind that Buddhism leads one to is exactly what is necessary for the creative process. Their education in Buddhism, which began at Naropa, was more or less an unfolding of an understanding of practical mental techniques. In order to become an improvising musician, capable of spontaneous creation of an original sound, one must enter a mental state that is not at all dissimilar to that of the Buddhist meditators. Far from being a "holy trip," as Ingrid explains, Buddhist mental discipline provides a useful tool for expressing one's self more truthfully and completely.

The extraordinary lama Kalu Rinpoche, who visited and taught at CMS, talked of the process in terms of *liberation through sound*, a concept that is central to music-universe, music-mind thinking. His presence at CMS was one of many outstanding events that characterized the intensification of associations with Tibetan masters at CMS, subsequent to the Naropa trips. It was Kalu's chief assistant, lama Norlha, who guided the establishment of a meditation room and basic meditation practice at CMS. Norlha later established his own center, twenty miles south of Woodstock.

After the founding in Woodstock of the Karma Triyana Dharmachakra, the monastery and American seat of His Holiness the Karmapa, informal visits from the Karmapa's lamas became a regular occurrence at CMS. A reciprocal relationship developed between CMS and the KTD that produced several benefit concerts and even a birthday festival for the Karmapa on the CMS grounds.

Karl refers to the numerous contacts with Tibetan Buddhists throughout CMS's history as "miraculous happenings" and claims that they easily could provide material enough for another entire book.

Tom Schmidt, Naropa Institute, Boulder, Colorado, 1975.

6

Mt. Tremper

"CMS was part of the process of allowing me to find out who I was."
—George Lewis

I remember vividly my approach to Mt. Tremper in the year of the Bicentennial, 1976. I was driving a 1966 Plymouth Fury, loaded with my drums, clothes, sheets and blankets, and whatever else I would need for a stay of what ended up being seven months. It was early March, and the leafless, wintry trees lent the Catskills a muted gray hue. Even so, the enchantment that Olatunji later described—that feeling of exiting the urban jungle, the miles of freeway, and the noise of the make-a-living world to enter this fairy land—was all over me.

I remember turning into the long gravel driveway at the Mt. Tremper site, thinking, "This can't be it! This is the middle of nowhere." I was used to institutions. I was used to the University of Michigan and such places. You get brochures and literature in the mail, you make application, you pay your money, and you go to the *institution.* This was like going out of time. Nothing could have prepared me for the aura of that building and its grounds. If I had been told that the Creative Music Studio was housed in an old, stone church (and I hadn't been), I still couldn't have pictured this. The building reminded me more of the giant's castle at the top of Jack's beanstalk than of a house of worship. It was kind of eerie, but kind of beautiful.

Part of that eeriness came from the fact that no one was there. Mine was the only car in the lot. Where was the smiling staff to greet me and say, "Welcome to CMS! Let me get you registered and show you to your room"? Where were all the other students, eager to get acquainted and get down to the business of learning and playing music?

I looked around and waited. Eventually, Tom Schmidt showed up; a few other students showed up. Tom explained that, yes, we were in the right place, and we were there at the right time. Karl would be along later to welcome and orient people, and our rooms are wherever we claim them.

After getting settled, meeting Karl Berger, and hearing of what was in store, I started to become aware that I was learning a very important lesson: Whatever expectations I had of what was to be my experience at CMS would have to be abandoned quickly. This was not to be an educational experience like any I had previously known. There would be no required classes, no exams, no grades in our eight-week program. Even the schedule of workshops was uncertain and likely to change at any time.

What there would be were opportunities that arise from being thrown together with some of the greatest improvising musicians on the planet. The weeks to come would bring us together with Dave Holland, Ed Blackwell, Sam Rivers, Don Cherry, Leo Smith, Oliver Lake, Richard Teitelbaum, and many others. This was an environment, though, that demanded maturity and creativity. It was up to each individual to make of the opportunities what he or she would. Show up at sessions or don't; practice the concepts and techniques that are being unveiled or don't; make contact with other musicians (students or guiding artists) and create ensembles and playing situations or don't.

We could participate in dancer Sara Cook's body-awareness sessions and nurture the body-mind relationship, which is vital to musicianship. We could develop rapport with other musicians that might develop into lifelong professional or personal gain. We could study traditional music theory. We could arrange for private lessons. We could get gigs with local musicians in and around Woodstock. We could play! We could really play—day in and day out, all night long if we could find a place where we wouldn't keep people awake. The opportunities were endless.

"One thing I'll always be thankful for and remember is that I got to meet a lot of really great musicians at that time in my life that I never would have met, probably, even if I had been in New York City."
—Donnie Davis

Some were able to do it all and thrive. Others, such as the individual who stormed into Karl's office and cried out, "There's too much freedom here!" were nearly helpless in such an environment. I remember one drummer, a blonde, beach-boy sort of guy who had come out from Ohio with his blonde, beach-boy sort of dad in his dad's new van. He was a big Buddy Rich fan, who had been to big-band camps in previous summers and was looking for more of the same experience. He and his dad took a quick look around, put his drums back in the van and headed back to Ohio. CMS was not for everybody.

John Lindberg

On the other hand, there was John Lindberg, whom I call the quintessential CMS student. John is a bassist, whose family moved from the Detroit area to Marshall, Michigan, when he was twelve. At that time, Roscoe Mitchell was living on a farm near Bath, Michigan, and doing concerts at Michigan State University, where John first saw him. John was so taken with Roscoe's performance that he asked him if he could become his student—a pretty fearless and advanced move for a kid who then was only fifteen! John soon after began working on Roscoe's farm and studying music with him. And soon after that, Roscoe suggested that he go to the Creative Music Studio.

"Being an adolescent, and a compulsive adolescent," John recalls, "I just got absorbed in the music, and all I wanted to do was just practice all the time and play. So this leads up to the decision to go to CMS. I was so obsessive with the music thing and studying with Roscoe, and I just wanted to practice eight or ten hours a day. I had a bass teacher over in Battle Creek, a guy named Mike Steiner from the Battle Creek Symphony. I was having those two lessons a week, and I told my parents, 'I don't have time to go to high school anymore. I've got all these things that I've gotta do on the bass.'"

John called Karl Berger and told him that he really wanted to come to CMS, but his parents were requiring him to finish high school. Karl put John in touch with Onteora High School, and they were able to work out an arrangement that allowed John to go to high school in the morning and return to Mount Tremper for CMS sessions in the afternoon. John was also able to arrange a private bass lesson with Dave Holland once a week.

"I was living there in that monastery in Mount Tremper," John says, "and the school bus would come and stop in front of the monastery at seven in the morning. I would get on and go into Woodstock to my high-school classes until noon, and then the bus would bring me back. I think I went about three days, and I said, 'Man, I don't have time to get up and go to this school thing.' I was hanging out with guys and we were playing until three in the morning. I stopped getting on the bus."

One of the guys that John was doing a lot of playing with was guitarist James Emery. James had recently come to New York from Ohio and got right into the scene working with Kalaparusha Ara Difda (Maurice McIntyre), Leroy Jenkins, and others. Karl heard James in a concert in Woodstock with Kalaparusha and asked him to come to CMS to teach guitar.

James and John discovered an affinity for each other's playing that kept them playing for sometimes eight hours a day. They later hooked up with violinist Billy Bang to form the String Trio of New York, an ensemble that has survived and still thrives, eighteen years later. The violin spot has changed from Billy Bang to Charles Burnham to Regina Carter at present, but James and John have remained tight. They've recorded thirteen albums and played in twenty-five countries.

What's unique about John Lindberg, though, is that his only institutional education has been at CMS, as institutional as that is. He never even finished high school. Yet this hasn't hindered him from establishing a busy and successful presence in creative music.

Creative Anarchy and Jack DeJohnette

CMS presented an environment that has been described as "creative anarchy." Things were often not what students expected them to be and, naturally, there were disappointments. The strongest thing drawing me to CMS was the name Jack DeJohnette, which seemed to appear on everything I read about the Studio. I had heard Jack on Miles Davis's "Live Evil" album, which I listened to inside and out—I had to keep listening to convince myself that this was, indeed, only one drummer. I had heard Jack also on Charles Lloyd and Jackie Maclean records. To be able to spend time with Jack DeJohnette would be an opportunity of a lifetime. I was told soon after arriving, however, that Jack would not be around in this spring 1976 session. I felt ripped off. There were many assurances, though, that this would be a great session with many fantastic people (and it was). Still, I was let down.

Someone (probably Karl) soon offered me Jack's phone number and the suggestion that I call him for private lessons. It was not easy to get hold of Jack and harder, still, to schedule a lesson. Several weeks went by before it happened. At the first lesson, Jack asked me if I had a dependable car. Sure, the Plymouth was dependable. He asked me if I wanted to drive him to Quebec City, Quebec, and be a roadie for a concert with the Gateway Trio (Jack, John Abercrombie on guitar,

Oliver Lake, Mt. Tremper, New York, 1976.

*Leo Smith, Mt.
Tremper, New
York, 1976.*

and Dave Holland on bass). Yes, of course I did. This is the type of opportunity for a drummer that only a fool would turn down.

The drive from Woodstock was about ten hours—ten hours of drum lesson, drum history, and stories of the jazz life with one of the greatest. We listened to a lot of music on that trip. That's when I began to learn how important it is to just listen to music with an experienced musician. See what he reacts to. Hear what he calls your attention to. Feel what gets him enthused.

John Abercrombie made the return trip with us. (I knew I liked the guy when I heard him tell a young Canadian admirer, only partly in jest, that one of his main influences was Chuck Berry.) I'll never forget that trip to and from Quebec City.

Throughout the summer I continued to work for Jack in exchange for lessons. Work might mean driving him to recording sessions to carry and set up his drums, or it might mean clearing his garden of the rocks that seem to be everywhere in the Catskills.

I met so many people with Jack, learned so much, and saw so much that the experience could not possibly compare with the Jack DeJohnette CMS workshops that I had earlier anticipated and subsequently felt deprived of. That was the point; that was the magic of the CMS experience. The more expectations one had, the greater the possibility one would be disappointed by the creative anarchy. Expectations were a burden. To be alert to what was going on when it was going on, to be open to the opportunities that were there and to make the most of them, that was the real lesson. We were learning not just music, but also to grow as people, to get beyond the smallness of our egos and discover our potential.

Outdoors with Don Cherry and Bob Moses

Don Cherry came one day, and we all sat out on the lawn in the sun. What transpired was the type of transference of music, stories, and vital information that has been part of all cultures of the world since the beginning of time.

Don told stories. He sang. We sang. He played and we played. He taught in the oral tradition of cultures untouched by or unconcerned with technology and mass communications. What made our experience different, though, from that of musicians whose heritage is traditionally passed down orally, was that our teacher was drawing not from the pool of a singular ethnic or cultural group, but from a wealth of knowledge from all over the earth and from all times.

Don Cherry's perspective is that of one who has studied in Africa, India, Europe, South America, and Asia. In each place he has picked up the music of the local people and somehow made it his own—blended it with his own background in American jazz music and come up with a world music that is unique. This session on the lawn brought me my first exposure to the Indian concept of assigning syllables to complex rhythm cycles. It was also my first opportunity to witness the frustration of experienced wind players as they tried to get anything resembling music out of the extremely difficult-to-play Japanese shakuhachi flute.

The grounds at Mt. Tremper seemed to have something magical about them, and everyone seemed to want to take full advantage of warm, sunny days by playing outside. Drummer Bob Moses jumped at the chance to take all of the drummers outside for his workshop. He had an energy level that no indoor space could contain, anyway. We took a group of eight or ten drummers out onto the lawn and soon had a solid, rolling, 9/8 groove going. The sun beat down, people were dancing. It was irresistible. There was a film crew there from Canada, recording it all as part of their CMS documentary. And then it started to rain—without a cloud in the sky! This wasn't just a drizzle, either. It rained hard enough that people scrambled for cover. Most of us kept on playing, and after about five minutes it stopped. Ask Bob Moses about it. To this day, he'll swear that we made it rain.

7

Oehler's Mountain Lodge

"I was successful by teaching there and being able to work out how to look at what I was dealing with with my system. I know the same thing was true with Anthony Braxton. All of us, everybody, instructors and so-called students, were able to get into a great deal of research that benefitted other musicians."

—Leo Smith

The Mt. Tremper location had a lot going for it aesthetically, but it was not a practical facility to try to maintain. It was a nightmare to heat in the winter, and the Lutherans wanted it back in the summer for day camp. CMS was growing and it needed its own home. The student population was increasing (the Studio at this point had hosted students from all fifty states and fifteen different countries), and the year-round schedule of workshops made the portable CMS concept less and less viable.

By 1976 a yearly cycle had taken hold, which consisted of a ten-day, new-year's intensive; an eight-week spring session; a summer intensive of ten days or two weeks; and a fall session of eight weeks. Articles in *Down Beat* and Japan's *Swing Journal* had brought CMS to the attention of the world, signifying it as a gathering place for some of the world's finest improvising and contemporary classical musicians.

The search for more permanent quarters led to Oehler's Mountain Lodge, an idyllic Catskill vacation resort in West Hurley, between Woodstock and Kingston. Oehler's consisted of a main lodge with residence rooms, office space, rooms for practicing, a huge kitchen and dining room, a main hall for performances and workshops, and a bar complete with juke box and pool table.

On the grounds there was a number of small cabins and two low, long, motel-like housing units. Two features of the resort that might have seemed incongruous and superfluous, yet really added to Oehler's appeal, were the Olympic-sized soccer field and swimming pool.

Eatin' with the Oehlers

The Creative Music Foundation entered into a rental agreement with the Oehler family, moved in, and held its first session there in the fall of 1976. On hand as guiding artists were Karl Berger, Ingrid Berger, Dave Holland, Steve Haas, Sara Cook, Anthony Braxton, Frederic Rzewski, Larry Chernicoff, Michael Gregory Jackson, Kalaparusha, and Oliver Lake. And, as saxophonist and long-time CMS student/worker Tom Collins recalls, "There was a great group of students that came, of various levels of proficiency, but the spirit was really great."

What made this session particularly odd, though, was that Mr. Oehler was still maintaining his business at the same time that CMS was in residence. Karl describes the arrangement as "a horrible deal. We had to buy their food. They were actually cooking—serving all this meat and beef and pork that nobody wanted—and running the bar. It was a disaster. They were in the middle. They were living there. Every morning when I would come in, I would see the old guy, Oehler, sitting there writing bills for us. He always ended up with $1,500 a week or $,2000 a week, amounts like that!"

Tom Collins portrays the juxtaposition of the two elements—the Oehlers with their mostly German, Catskill-resort clientele and the "counter-culture, hippie, young, avant-garde music people"—as bizarre. "They had the World War II submarine veterans holding their convention there. We never figured out which veterans they were, whether they were Germans or Americans—I have a feeling they were German submarine veterans that were all living in the United States. And then there was the German-American soccer group and CMS all there at the same time at one point." Many of the CMS people were vegetarians who found sharing a menu with the submarine veterans to be one of the less appealing parts of their CMS experience. "Mrs. Oehler cooked the food. 'Eggs, any style'—I'll never forget that. And once a week they'd have French toast, except it was German toast. It was deep fried. You'd cut into it and oil would ooze out. They also served canned vegetables. There was lots of it, though, they didn't scrimp on the food."

In Walked Marianne

A standard feature of the long sessions was a student concert every week. Guiding artists would work with a student ensemble for a week, and at the end of the week, usually a Friday, there would be a student concert open to the public.

According to Tom and his wife Marianne, the occasion of Oliver Lake's concert, November 6, 1976, was a particularly surreal night at Oehler's. Tom was a member of the student orchestra and describes an extended piece of Oliver's, which was performed that night: "In rehearsal, there was one little section of the piece, where the instruction was everyone play as loud and as fast as you can. And in rehearsal it was about twenty seconds. It was the whole ensemble, about twenty-two various instruments, a lot of saxophones, a couple piano players, one bass, and five drummers—you know, the usual CMS ensemble. When it came to the concert, he [Oliver] hit it . . . and he just left it there. And it went on and on and on. I would say it went on twenty minutes. It was quite an experience. Later, Oliver said he just thought he would see what would happen."

"So that ended," Marianne remembers, "and you'd walk out of this experience that was somewhat mind boggling and into the bar with the World War II sub vets and the oom-pah-pah music on the juke box. It was *very* bizarre."

Tom recalls, "They were all going, 'I don't know what this shit is! I don't know what this shit is! I like jazz. I used to like jazz. This isn't jazz. I don't know what this shit is! This is the worst shit I ever heard!'"

"And there was this very elderly, little, old, inebriated German guy," continues Marianne, "who would sit there with his dog named Hans or Heinz or something, and the dog would wear a wig. It was a true surreal experience."

Marianne, who was Marianne Boggs at the time, was visiting CMS for the first or second time. Although she had a solid background in music (She had sung her way through college, earning good money as a folk singer) and loved all types of music, nothing in her experience had prepared her for what she heard at CMS. She told me, "I had never heard anything like this in my entire life. I thought this was the most horrendous thing I had ever experienced. It made no sense to me, musically; and I remember thinking this is a joke . . . and I don't get it. . . . But it was also fascinating. I was listening and hearing things; but I just didn't know what was going on."

Later, in the spring of 1977, Marianne was asked to write an arts column for a Woodstock Chamber of Commerce booklet. This led her back to CMS, this time to interview Karl Berger. "I thought, aha, this is my chance to find out what the hell those people are doing.

"I walked in and he [Karl] said, 'Oh I remember you. You were at three of the concerts last year.' And I thought that it was really amusing—I didn't remember him. It was another bizarre reversal where the musicians could actually remember the audience because they were so few in number. . . .

"I asked him what was the purpose, what was the concept, what was the format, why would that man leave those musicians making all that noise for twenty minutes? So, he told me all about it, and it made perfect sense. Conceptually, it made perfect sense—what they were trying to do, what the point was. At that point I don't think that world music had begun to emerge as a concept in his mix. It was really more contemporary classical and jazz and the extensions."

The next day, Marianne got a call from Ben Patterson asking her to come to work for the Creative Music Foundation. Ben Patterson had become a part of the organization in mid-1976. He was a classical bassist, but also someone with a good deal of administrative and fund-raising experience. He had created the "Composer in Performance" series, which later became "Meet the Composer."

According to Marianne, "He was very impressive—almost a James Earl Jones kind of presence. He was a fine intellect and had sort of a large person with a large voice. He was quite a visionary—different from Karl. But you could see that bringing the two of them together could be quite dynamic."

Before Ben Patterson and Marianne Collins, nearly all of the administration, fund raising, and public relations for CMS had been taken on by people who had come as students, saw the need, and took the work on. Some came with skills, but others learned their jobs from scratch. Larry Chernicoff knew nothing about graphics before he began putting together flyers and posters. After some years of creating weekly announcements for concerts and workshops, he had learned enough to start his own graphics and design business. Ilene Marder learned grant writing and administration from the ground up—skills that served her in several subsequent positions, including one with Woodstock Ventures, the group that put on the major Woodstock festivals.

Having two full-time administrators marked a turning point for CMS. This was the first time that the Studio had people at the top who were not there primarily to study music. Students still worked in administrative capacities (work-study arrangements), and their help

Don Cherry, Woodstock, New York, 1976 or 1977.

*Bob Moses,
Studio Rivbea,
New York
City, 1973.*

remained critical throughout the life of CMS.

Marianne jokes that her entry into this inner circle came about in part because "they [Karl and Ben Patterson] had very accurately judged that I would be the last one to say, 'What does it pay?' And, actually, I never did find out—because it never did." She goes on to say, "When I walked in, the few people who were working there . . . all looked at me like, who is this person? She must really be a fool. You could get the vibes. [They were thinking] she's not here because she wants to musically express herself . . . and there ain't no money. What is she doing here?

"The day I came to work [in May of 1977], the entire music department of the New York State Council on the Arts was there— James Jordan [Ornette Coleman's cousin, who was a valued liaison with NYSCA] and all these music people who were reviewing the place for a grant. It looked pretty impressive. And then they left. And then everybody left. Ben left and there was no money, and there were bills owed. And suddenly I was on the phone explaining to people—or not explaining, because I didn't really know why there was no money to pay them for whatever it was that we had just ordered and gotten delivered."

The time that Marianne and Ben Patterson worked together was actually quite short, perhaps a month or two. It wasn't long before she assumed (or was consumed by) the role of administrative director of the Creative Music Foundation. "My role," she recalls, "evolved fairly quickly from just trying to figure out how you get students from not knowing anything about it [CMS] to having them fully enrolled. We called that the 'you fit the bill, you foot the bill' concept. It took me a long time to figure out the financial needs that drove some of the policies. When great ideas are not financially well supported, they start to sort of rot. For all the time I was there, it was really an attempt to support good ideas and good work and terrific talent with the kind of financing that it took. I went from really knowing nothing about it, knowing nothing about operating a business, to having some amazing successes. All of our NEA [National Endowment for the Arts] funding grew up while I was there. I quickly became the administrative director and treasurer of the foundation.

"I can't even recall how it happened; it was just sort of a series of boom, boom, boom. It was a matter of grant writing, bringing in money for programs, refining the sessions so that they were a little balanced and could be responsive depending on what kinds of musical instruments were there. [I] was really trying to put a little more structure to it and a little more of a planning process to it than had been possible before. Because, in truth, the only people who had been in there before were really committed to their own musical expression first and then tried to deal with the institution and the institutional structure."

8

Settling In

"Seeing the way that . . . Karl and Braxton and Dave Holland and people like that operated and committed themselves to music was a good example for me. It showed me that it could be done if you worked hard enough and believed in yourself enough, that you could really make a career out of it, as well as a life, a calling."
— James Emery

Although the financial responsibility of maintaining Oehler's Mountain Lodge (which the Creative Music Foundation ended up buying) contributed a great deal to the Studio's ultimate downfall, having a home of its own gave CMS a strong boost. It allowed an expansion. Everything seemed to get bigger. The student body continued to grow; public awareness of the Studio attracted more numerous and diverse guiding artists; the administrators' fund-raising skills grew; the concert series grew; and there was an overall sense of momentum.

As the Studio and its programs matured, Karl was able to draw more master improvisers from Africa, Turkey, India, Asia, and South America. This increase in international involvement culminated in large-scale, world-music summer festivals in 1979, 1980, 1981, and 1982.

There is little documentation available on CMS activities in 1977. The big news for that year was, of course, the purchase of Oehler's. A tremendous amount of energy went into securing the funds needed for the deal. However, a look at the program catalogs for the year conveys a sense of what it must have been like to be a part of CMS.

So called avant-garde jazz, free jazz, new jazz was in its heyday, and CMS continued to attract the cream of the crop. The "contemporary classicists" were also represented in the figures of Frederic Rzewski and William Ames. Yet, links to jazz's traditions and its mainstream were preserved at CMS by workshops with legends Jimmy Giuffre and Lee Konitz.

Those who know saxophonist/clarinetist/flutist Jimmy Giuffre from his days in the swing era with Woody Herman and who associate his sound with the smoothness of the Four Brothers might be surprised to find him in the company of players such as Oliver Lake, Leo Smith, Anthony Braxton, et al. But Giuffre was no stranger to freer, more forward-looking concepts.

In the fifties he came together with Ornette Coleman while teaching at the Lenox (Massachusetts) School of Jazz. He recalls that Ornette was "assigned" to him, because he (Giuffre) was teaching clarinet and saxophone. "He wrote so fast," says Giuffre, "that the stems of his notes were to the right, like the wind had blown them. Everything he wrote was like that."

The boundaries between student and teacher became rather fuzzy, though, as they often did at CMS and in many situations where creative music is exchanged. Giuffre says that "at that time [Ornette] had done some very important things. He was unique. People looked up to him and with good reason. . . . We had a momentous session with him, George Russell, Bags [Milt Jackson], and Percy Heath. . . . They were playing 'Lullabye of the Leaves,' and I couldn't find out what they were doing, so I sat out. But I was encouraged to go back and try some more. . . . Something happened on that night that really turned me on."

1977

The 1976-1977 New Year's Intensive brought students together with Karl and Ingrid Berger, Barry Altschul, Charles Brackeen, Jimmy Giuffre, Garrett List, Sam Rivers, James Blood Ulmer, Ed Blackwell, Dave Holland, David Izenson, Michael Gregory Jackson, Lee Konitz, Paul Motian, and Leo Smith. The winter session (January to March) presented that same lineup plus Don Cherry, Steve Haas, Leroy Jenkins, Oliver Lake, Michael Manieri, Jumma Santos, Muhal Richard Abrams, William Ames, Warren Bernhardt, Anthony Braxton, Kalaparusha, Steve Lacy, Frederic Rzewski, and the Woodstock Dance Ensemble.

Karl put on a CMS benefit concert in January at Boston's Church of the Covenant, which the *Boston Evening Globe* called "a model of its kind. . . . It had taste, shape, and an adventuresome variety. But the event had also had a charm and style that generated a pervasive good feeling among the artists and the 700 or so in the audience."[1]

---

1. Ray Murphy, "'Alternative Jazz' Points to New Directions," *Boston Evening Globe,* January 21, 1977, p. 20.

Part of the "adventuresome variety" was due to the groupings of the musicians who performed. Karl and Ingrid were joined by Oliver Lake, Ed Blackwell, Jimmy Giuffre, and bassist Patty Preiss. Steve Gorn, a specialist in North Indian Classical music and the premier western player of the bansuri flute also performed. Steve later did a number of workshops at CMS in which he taught modal, melodic improvisation based on Indian ragas. Michael Gregory Jackson and Oliver Lake did duets. Pianist Anthony Davis was there, and guitarist Baird Hersey performed his piece "Creation and Holocaust" with a rhythm section and twenty-five saxophones.

In February, Karl performed "Cycles" in Albany, New York, with Electronic Body Arts, an Albany modern dance company. Karl played solo piano, electric piano, and vibraphone with various groupings of the six dancers. According to the *Schenectady Gazette*, Karl "played effortlessly, with sensitivity and clarity. His improvisations soared and searched but never wandered too far from their sweetly melodic base."[2]

Peter Apfelbaum and Marilyn Crispell

There have been so many outstanding creative musicians who came to CMS—too many to go on about at length. But two who came in the summer and fall of 1977, Peter Apfelbaum and Marilyn Crispell, deserve a special mention for the marks they made on the CMS scene while they were there and on the professional creative-music scene since then.

Peter Apfelbaum of Berkeley, California, was one of the youngest players to come to CMS. He is now a seasoned veteran, having collaborated with Don Cherry and others and having spent over eighteen years with his own large group, the Hieroglyphics Ensemble.

Peter began drum lessons at the age of five, was playing piano by the age of ten, and picked up the saxophone at the age of eleven. By the time he got to CMS he was seventeen and playing all three well enough to make a lot of folks sit up and take notice. Here was a kid who appeared to be primarily a saxophone player, yet he was putting many of the more experienced drummers to shame. He, like John Lindberg, the bassist, had introduced himself to the Art Ensemble of Chicago at a very tender age—thirteen.

"I started music very young," Peter told me. "I started when I

2. Peg Churchill, "EBA Underlines Its Claim to Quality with 'Cycles'," *Schenectady Gazette*, February 22, 1977.

was in preschool. The teacher had kind of a progressive approach, and she would encourage kids to focus on creative things if that's what they wanted to do. I always went over to the corner where the drums were.

"Early on I was spending a lot of time working with instruments and sounds; I don't know what drew me in. . . . I was able to benefit from a real strong music education program here in the [Berkeley] public schools. In 1966, Herb Wong, who has written some books on jazz and had been a jazz DJ, was at that time a principal of an elementary school. He had the foresight and whatever it took to start and implement a jazz program. He recruited Dick Whittington, a jazz pianist who's still here in the Bay Area; he came up from L.A. He was my piano teacher at one point when I was twelve or thirteen. He and a man named Phil Hardiman managed to do really great things with young kids in introducing them to jazz, and I was one of the first to be able to take advantage of that program.

"David Murray was there, too. He was in the school band. And there was a pianist there named Rodney Franklin. He and I played together a lot when we were kids, but by the time we were teenagers we went our separate ways, because we musically had real different goals. But there were a lot of talented kids . . . like Benny Green, Craig Handy. And even after I graduated, some of my students went through there, like Josh Redman.

"When I was thirteen, I had a gig with this pianist Dick Whittington, and I learned the standards, and I learned blues. . . . I got to really learn the jazz repertoire. But what was really captivating me and really moving me was people like Cecil [Taylor], and Sun Ra, and Don [Cherry], and Pharaoh Sanders. The Art Ensemble of Chicago came out here for the first time in 1973. They opened for Charles Mingus at the Berkeley Community Theater. . . .

"I was exposed to some things that I wouldn't have been exposed to if I hadn't been in Berkeley. It's thanks to the Bay Area and the idea that Herb Wong had and the whole jazz program that's part of it. But it's also the fact that the Bay Area itself is both very multicultural and it's also very progressive politically and socially. And I think that's one reason that I really related to both CMS and Woodstock.

"The people who were teaching there [summer 1977] were Karl and Ingrid, of course, and Carla Bley was there, Michael Mantler [who was teaching a class on the music business], Garrett List, the trombonist. Abdullah Ibrahim came up for a few days. Leo Smith was there, Jimmy Giuffre. I guess Sunny Murray was there around that time. So these were the types of people who were teaching there then. And, boy, it was really interesting. It's hard to know where to start.

"For an artist in this society to survive and construct their life in such a way so that it works for them is a really challenging thing. It really keeps you guessing. It's so valuable for artists to learn from other artists, how they live—just day to day things. For me to find out those things was crucial. You can only learn so much from your parents, and you can only learn so much from school. If you're in music, and if you're in this type of music, which involves creativity and involves thinking and interacting with people—and at the same time finding a way to deal with other things later on, like poverty and obscurity and. . . get[ting] your projects realized, you really have to find out from other artists how they do it. Because society doesn't give you any kind of manual on how to live as an artist.

"That's one of the reasons why CMS was so important. I got to talk to musicians not only about their music . . . but I was exposed to all these people that were making decisions and doing other things that kept them going, other things that had spiritual sustenance for them—like Buddhism. It was the first time that I had gotten exposed to certain Buddhist concepts, through Karl and Ingrid, and through Joseph [Jarman], actually. That time that they [the Art Ensemble of Chicago] came, he gave me this book called *Light on the Path*.

"At [one] point, I had a lot of horns with me; I had my alto, tenor, a C soprano, and I had gotten a bass saxophone, which was in disrepair. I had all this stuff there, and I wasn't playing it all. And one day, I was walking somewhere, outside the dining hall, or somewhere, and Roscoe [Mitchell] walked by. He said, 'Hey Peter, go get your bass saxophone. We're gonna go to the repair shop.' I said, 'Oh, yeah?' And he said, 'Yeah, come on. I'll pay for it. We gotta get that thing fixed.'

"So I went and got my bass saxophone and jumped in the car with him, no questions asked. He had found out about this little music shop that was way out in the woods. It was near one of these little, little towns. This guy had a little music studio that was like a shack out in the middle of nowhere. Once we got out there, I don't know if Roscoe even had any business of his own to take care of. It didn't seem like it. He was really just being generous with his time. Unfortunately, the guy looked at the bass saxophone and didn't think that he could do anything with it. The body had been bent, and later on I had to spend more money and get it fixed somewhere else.

"But the fact of the matter was that Roscoe was so generous in offering to do that. It was about a half hour's drive, and we just talked. We talked about everything. We talked about music, we talked about women, we talked about politics, we talked about jazz promoters—who to avoid and things like that.

"That [type of experience] was something that was pretty much unique to CMS. . . . CMS was really filling a void. And for people like me, who were into creative music and its different forms and the different ways that people would organize their music, it was incredible. Being a composer, I was interested in composing. When I went out there, the Hieroglyphics Ensemble had already been formed, and I was trying out some of my compositions, although they were rather embryonic at the time. But being at CMS, I was able to see how people were reconstructing. [Anthony] Braxton used the term *restructuralist* . . . , which I think is a great word. It identifies the musicians who—once things got blown apart in the sixties, conventions got blown apart, and the focus was more on spontaneous creation of music—, like the Chicago people [Association for the Advancement of Creative Musicians], were at the forefront of picking up the pieces and putting them together in new ways.

"A lot of these restructuralists were people that we got to study with—people like Braxton. Although I didn't get to study with him at that time, I got to see his music, because he was living in Woodstock and he had a giant orchestra piece that he was working on. He had to hire a lot of people to help him copy it out. At one point at the Creative Music Studio, there were maybe ten or twelve people that were always working like elves in little corners of the Creative Music Studio on this Braxton piece. He could just walk through and see parts at various stages of completion. That was something I got to check out in a very informal way.

"And then [there was] Abdullah Ibrahim, who wouldn't write any of his music down. He does it by oral tradition, the way that a lot of African musicians like to teach their music. We'd hear it and have to get it from hearing it, and develop our memories more. And then the way Cecil [Taylor] does it—he'll show you things, or he'll write things down. He'll write down the names of the notes, and you'll develop the rhythm over rehearsing. And then Michael Mantler—he's a little bit more conventional in his notation. But he uses these brackets to signal various things, repeats and such. Leo Smith has this thing that he developed called *rhythm units*. One of the things that Leo said that stuck with me was something to the effect that to fully hear and appreciate a musical phrase, you have to let enough space go by after the phrase, to really hear it back. So, we would do experiments where we would play, and then let roughly the same amount of time as what we had played go by in silence. . . . The point is, I got to learn things about the structure of music that I couldn't have gotten anywhere else."

Pianist Marilyn Crispell was one of a select few CMS students who came with a strong background in formal music education. She had graduated from Boston's New England Conservatory of Music in 1968 with a degree in applied piano. Before coming to CMS, Marilyn was working in Boston as an accompanist for dancers, a situation that allowed to her improvise, but wasn't in a style that was "100 percent jazz—or jazz at all." There were similarities, though, in that she was using fourth-chord voicings similar to what she found in McCoy Tyner's playing. She became exposed to jazz around 1973 and began studying the traditional jazz repertoire around 1975 with a teacher named Charley Banacos, who was at the Berklee College of Music at the time. Her exposure to most of the musicians who were teaching at CMS had been minimal. Nonetheless, she came to CMS with a sense of purpose and a determination to launch herself to a new level professionally. "I knew that I was ready to do something," Marilyn recalls, "and I knew that I would meet the people there who I would be able to do things with. . . . It couldn't have happened without that situation."

She hadn't been there long when she attracted the attention of Anthony Braxton. Marilyn was rehearsing an orchestra piece that George Russel was preparing for the student orchestra, and Anthony happened to hear her—and liked what he heard. Soon after that, Marilyn found herself performing a duo concert with Anthony, at the conclusion of which he announced, "This is my new pianist." Marilyn "kind of took it with a grain of salt," but did, indeed, become Anthony Braxton's new pianist. That collaboration has continued now for over fifteen years, although they have worked together less frequently in recent years.

Cecil Taylor also just happened to hear Marilyn play, and he, too, took note. This, though, was more of a contrived happenstance. Cecil was playing pool in the bar at Oehler's. By this time (winter 1980), the bar was just a room with a pool table. Liquor sales had stopped when the Oehlers moved out, but a good deal of Oehler's liquor was still stored in the basement. Certain devious rascals discovered this cache and were able to "spirit" a good deal of it away. These same characters also discovered that they could play pool forever, without putting more coins in, by putting styrofoam cups in the pockets to catch the balls. The man who collected the coins for the company that owned the table discovered this one day, and that was the end of the pool table at CMS. But that's all another story.

Marilyn says that she saw Cecil playing pool and that she had "this incredible desire to have him hear me play." Without saying anything to him, she went into one of the two practice rooms adjacent to the bar and played a little concert. He listened to the whole thing, and when she came out, he kissed her hand. That was how she met Cecil Taylor. This sort of accessibility to musicians of the stature of Cecil Taylor, Anthony Braxton, and so many others was what made CMS unique.

Marilyn acknowledges that "it was incredible that you could meet so many different types of musicians there." If one were to go to New York City to try to get to know these people by going to the clubs where they play or trying to interrupt their busy schedules, it might never happen.

CMS was a "revelation" to Marilyn in many ways. She regards the training she received with Don Cherry, for example, as extremely valuable. His style of teaching without notated music was as different from the conservatory approach as anything could be. Some students, like Marilyn, could adapt well and expand under his influence—actually, it was more like a spell that he cast. For others, though, their backgrounds or level of musicianship left them in the dark while trying to grasp his music. "His [approach] was all about listening," says Marilyn, "and I think that was really difficult for some people. But I wish there was more of that."

Leo Smith also took Marilyn and the others far from the conservatory in his way of working with the music. "He had a system that used written music and certain compositional concepts. At the same time, there was enough freedom and space where everyone's individuality could be expressed without a lot of difficulty. . . . With a minimum of effort he brought out the maximum of musicality."

Within a year of coming to CMS, Marilyn, herself, had begun teaching. Through improvisation, sight-reading, and ear-training classes, she was able to bridge the realms of classical and improvised musics. In her classes, jazz players were challenged by sight reading four-part Renaissance pieces. Players with a classical background were able to stretch and become better listeners and improvisers. Marilyn even taught Gregorian chants.

After a decade of working steadily with Anthony Braxton's quartet, Marilyn has a firm foothold as a professional, creative, performing and recording artist. These days, Marilyn is involved with a number of projects of her own that take her frequently to Europe to play with European musicians. She has also spent much time in the ensemble of renowned bassist Reggie Workman. Despite her status and all of her world-class experiences, she still says of her time at CMS, "I miss it immensely."

Sam Rivers, Studio Rivbea, New York City, 1973.

James Emery, New York City, 1974.

The Hurley Woods Festival

Having a relatively permanent home at Oehler's, particularly one with such spacious grounds, meant that CMS could initiate what would become a tradition of European-style (or Woodstock-style) summer arts and music festivals. The first of these, in the summer of 1977, was the Hurley Woods Festival, which combined a series of weekend concerts with a six-week "program for the study and performance of contemporary improvised and notated music."

The concerts were a fascinating mix of "artists from the Creative Music Studio, Speculum Musicae, the Schoenberg String Quartet, the Jazz Composers Orchestra Association, and the Hudson Valley Philharmonic, with special guests" (from a festival brochure). They blended together or performed separately, forming Festival Ensembles and the Festival Orchestra.

From duos, trios, quartets, full orchestra, and solo piano, the Hurley Woods absorbed the sounds of composers who were present to perform—Frederic Rzewski, Carla Bley, Michael Mantler, Garrett List, Karl Berger, Leo Smith—and those whom the performers chose to honor—Bartok, Brahms, Anton Webern, Edgar Varese, John Cage, Schoenberg, Dollar Brand (Abdullah Ibrahim), and William Ames. There were even Dixieland and Scott Joplin ensembles that were composed of members of the Hudson Valley Philharmonic.

The Hurley Woods Festival was the largest community outreach event that CMS had undertaken so far. It was important to Karl that CMS be a catalyst within the community, that it bring together audiences and performers from throughout the county and the greater Hudson Valley region. Through this festival and many to come, residents of the area came to be aware of artists and performers that they might not otherwise have heard of. There was (and is) a wealth of talent that many people in the area knew nothing about.

The fall of 1977 was more or less a continuation of what had begun earlier in the year. Many of the same artists returned for each of the '77 sessions. One new contributor that fall was dancer Raymond Johnson, who had performed at the Hurley Woods festival. Raymond had a dance company that has tragically all, including Raymond, been lost to AIDS. He and Sara Cook were both on hand that fall for dance, movement, and body awareness classes.

Michael Mantler taught a class on the music business, a topic that Jack DeJohnette's wife, Lydia, also presented in 1978 and 1979 sessions. Carla Bley brought her antics. "I just did a comedy act," she recalls. She would have everyone in the class pass their instruments to the person on their left and then play Christmas carols.

She also devised a *humatron*, which involved each person in the ensemble being assigned a specific note, one note only. Carla would then play the humatron by pointing to the person who was assigned the specific note that she wanted to hear. She also gained notoriety by instigating food fights, a little bit of fun that ultimately got her banned from the dining room.

Speaking of food, Carla has shed some light on the matter of whether American creative musicians are being deprived because of the need to perform in Europe, where they are more readily accepted. I asked her if she were bothered by this disparity, and she said, "no, not at all. I prefer the food in Europe. If you toured here, you'd be eating some horrible food."

The Art Ensemble of Chicago

The 1977-1978 New Year's Intensive session, however, was something altogether different. When I received notice in the mail at my home in Detroit that the Art Ensemble of Chicago would be in residence at CMS for ten days, I knew instantly that nothing would keep me from being there. It was one of those crystalline moments in life, in which there is not a shred of uncertainty. I can remember standing and looking at the brochure and feeling elated knowing that this experience was going to be mine.

No other group in the history of jazz (dare I say the history of music?) has been as successful at linking the ancient and the future. Their individual virtuosity is legendary. Their improvisational group interplay and fearless explorations of the limits of sonic expression have influenced, now, generations of improvisers around the world. The only group in jazz to rival their longevity is the Modern Jazz Quartet, which disbanded once and ceased to be modern long ago. The Art Ensemble had done numerous workshops in locations where they had come to perform, but they had never before done a residency that would put them under one roof with a student group for ten full days.

When it came time to leave Detroit for Woodstock that December, my car had broken down. Undaunted, I quickly switched my travel plans to Amtrak. The train was so much better, anyway. The ride, which delivered me to Rhinebeck, New York, had so much more of a feeling of adventure. This was the first time that I had had to deal with transporting my drums via public transportation. This was the first time that I had traveled as a musician in a mode other than the automobile. I was on top of the world.

It seems to me that it was Tom Cora, the cellist, who picked me up at the station in Rhinebeck a day or two before the session was to begin. As with any session, there was no lack of extra chores to be done. I soon found out that a volunteer was being sought to take a rented truck to Albany to pick up Joseph Jarman, Don Moye, and all of the Art Ensemble's equipment. Wait a minute! This is work? Do you think that there was any chance that I would pass up an opportunity to hang out, ride, and work (even in the capacity of roadie) with these two guys? Not on your life.

No explicit plans had been made to meet them. All I knew was their flight number and arrival time. Having seen the Art Ensemble in photographs and on album covers, though, I was sure that spotting them in an airport in Albany should be no problem. They were certain to stand out in any crowd.

Fortunately, the first person I spoke to, an airlines ticket agent, knew that they had retired to the cocktail lounge. Upon entering the lounge, I quickly noticed with more than a little surprise that the only two black men there were dressed in finely tailored Italian business suits! They looked sharp, cosmopolitan, a little like diplomats. They were Joseph Jarman and Don Moye.

I felt ridiculous greeting them in my army-surplus fatigue jacket and blue jeans. When I expressed my surprise at not seeing them in the African-inspired outfits that I was used to seeing them in, Jarman told me that traveling in the garb that they were most identified with as performers was not worth the hassle that they often received from airport and customs officials. They get to where they're going and then make their statement.

After loading what seemed to be a mountain of cases of instruments, luggage, and equipment, we began to make our way back to Woodstock. The intensive session had already begun for me. That ride was a demystifying and educational experience. It helped me to understand Jarman and Moye as people and to understand how the grunt work and glory of being a celebrated performer are often inseparable. It was a lesson in many things, including the logistics of moving a group and its equipment around the world (I believe that they had just flown in from Europe). An upcoming musician who is trying to make it has to learn many things. How to play his instrument is just one.

You will, however, learn a very great deal about playing your instrument if you have the opportunity to spend time with the Art

Ensemble of Chicago. Each member of the group held classes for his respective instrument group, which I suppose would be called master classes in the classical world—we were, after all, being taught by masters.

I attended Don Moye's classes for drummers, so I can't speak first hand of how the other classes went. Famoudou Don Moye brought to us certain African concepts applicable to the drum set that served me later in working with Roy Brooks' Aboriginal Percussion Choir in Detroit. We worked on playing individual parts that would be blended into an ensemble piece. And boy, did we work. For the better part of an hour at a time we would play pieces such as Don's "Baya." We would stop only when the rhythm started to fall apart. "Focus!" Don would command. "Keep your eyes open! Don't space *in!*"

One of the most intriguing things about Don Moye is that he can play with such intensity at such low volumes. He has to, to avoid completely drowning out Malachi Favors' unamplified bass. He explained to us how he used to practice so quietly that he could still hear whatever else was going on in a room.

"The baddest cats are playing close to the head," Don said one day. Any drummer who feels that his or her volume or dynamics are getting out of control would do well to keep that in mind.

I can recall walking by the room where Lester Bowie was working with brass players. They were making sounds with their mouthpieces alone that defied all conventional understanding of what a trumpet or trombone should sound like, or anything else, for that matter.

Reed players would have been put to the ultimate challenge in Roscoe Mitchell's class. It may surprise some who regard the Art Ensemble of Chicago as just a free-blowing group to know that Roscoe Mitchell worked to instill the highest technical proficiency in his students. Andrew Voigt, a San Francisco area saxophonist who went on to form the Rova Saxophone Quartet, studied privately with Roscoe and recalls a very demanding regimen. "We'd read anything and everything we could get our hands on," says Andrew. And they'd transpose into all twelve keys. Bass players were always scarce at CMS, so the one or two who were there would have had Maghostus Malachi Favors all to themselves.

In orchestra sessions, which included all students enrolled (and sometimes visitors), the various members of the Art Ensemble brought their distinctive approaches to unite the ensemble. Roscoe Mitchell's pieces required the most discipline and concentration. We worked for hours on his piece "Nonaah." The piece was cryptic. Written instructions and symbols were as prevalent as standard musical notation. Everyone wondered, at least at some point in the piece, what the heck we were supposed to be doing. Different sections of the orchestra would have to wait long periods of time while Roscoe straightened out other sections. Despite the frustration that many of us felt, there was an air of exhilaration in the room that came from knowing that we were working with one of the foremost composers to emerge from the evolution of jazz.

We played the blues with Malachi Favors. It was spirited and energized blowing—a thrill for such a large ensemble to be given free reign and still kept in check by the format of the blues. At one point our only instruction was to play blues in E—fast. (Don Cherry has said that are only three tempos: slow, medium, and fast. This was fast!) And it went on for a long time. Of course, no one works harder than the rhythm section in a situation like that. My right forearm felt like it was about to seize up when Malachi brought us all to halt. Later, he told me: "Yeah, you really held that, man." I still get a good feeling when I think about what those words meant to me at the time.

Lester Bowie led similar sessions, in which a rhythm was laid down and everyone got a chance to invent on top of it. Lester, though, was at that time experimenting with reggae music. So, rather than play the blues or something cerebral, we played reggae. You could always count on Lester for a good time.

"This is your life, and it's beautiful if you decide it to be so."
—Joseph Jarman

The high point of those ten days, at least in my memory and that of many whom I've spoken to, was the work that we did with Joseph Jarman. Joseph required each one of us to become a composer and to perform our compositions with an ensemble of our own construction. But it wasn't just music that we were to compose. Each composition, although short, had to contain a theatrical element. It was not enough to just play; we had to move, speak, act, use color, dance. We had to stretch our imaginations and really create something unique. It didn't matter whether or not we knew how to compose music in a traditional way.

Anyone with ideas can compose, Joseph stressed. You need only write down directions for the members of your group. It could be standard notation, or it could be instructions written in sentences. ("Play 'All the Things You Are' blindfolded, while the trombone player and the piano player argue over whether to play Canasta or Gin Rummy.") There were no limitations.

Day after day we came to the workshop with eager anticipation to see what our cohorts had come up with. Some pieces were brilliant;

some were ridiculous; some were hilarious; and some actually featured beautiful, moving, original music.

Joseph also integrated concepts from his many years of martial arts training into his message of complete human expression. He demonstrated to us all how fragile our physical balance really is by pointing out how much we actually quiver and vibrate while trying to stand perfectly still. His slightest touch would cause most of us to take steps to keep from falling. He further demonstrated the importance of mind and body integration by having each person project a note out to the most distant point he or she could imagine.

Most people responded by playing loud. "No, no, I didn't ask you to play *loud*," Joseph would remind them. "I asked you to *project*." It was as much a mental exercise as a physical one. He explained that these abilities—centering with balance, control of our instruments and their sounds, as well as endurance and the ability to focus to one task—could all be developed through the study of aikido, the Japanese art based on the fighting techniques of the samurai.

I was hooked. After returning to Detroit, I sought out an aikido class and began to study under Sensei Takashi Kushida. Now, after thirteen years of training, when asked how I began the study of aikido, I recount my time with Joseph Jarman at CMS. I'll always be grateful to him for helping me to understand that the application of harmony and focus is the same, whether in a musical ensemble, on the mat in the dojo, in the family, or on the job.

Joseph Jarman and Don Moye performed a duet concert at CMS on January 8, 1978, which they entitled "Egwu Anwu." It was recorded and released on the India Navigation label under the same title.

Unfortunately, the album could in no way capture the total experience of the evening. The costumes, the movement, the sounds, the colors, and the incense all worked together to transport the audience and fill us all with a sense of primal, ancient, and timeless Africa. It was spooky, actually.

I saw the duo perform the same concert later at New York University; at least one child in the audience started to cry when Jarman and Moye made their appearance, looking like spirits of the bush.

Several of us pitched in to help set up the labyrinth of equipment for the live recording: huge racks of sturdy piping for gongs of several sizes; Moye's personal, mutiple-percussion kit (drumset); tables of bells, shakers, chimes, whistles, woodblocks—small percussion instruments of every description; Jarman's saxophone's and flutes; and guideways for the great lengths of microphone cables. It was a big event and we all felt we were a part of it, not merely spectators.

The 1977-1978 New Year's Intensive session was so successful that the Art Ensemble was asked back to do the 1978-1979 New Year's Intensive. There is so little documentation of these two events that the memories of those who were there remain the best record. Unfortunately, after seventeen years, most of our memories have blurred the two intensive sessions together into one Art Ensemble of Chicago-at-CMS experience. It was an important, memorable time, not only for the students, but for the members of the Art Ensemble of Chicago.

Joseph Jarman recalls that it was a "great kind of experience, because the people accepted me, and I accepted them. They seemed to be interested in what I was about, and I was interested in what they were about. There was an air of mutual respect, which is kind of rare. And this makes it an event to remember, when you can feel people really trying— and those people were really trying. . . . Everybody [all the members of the Art Ensemble] got cooperation all the time . . . that's all they were ever after." By contrast, Joseph told of a workshop that they did at the University of California at Berkeley. "It was terrible," he recalls. Unlike at CMS, where the group was able to create and carry out its own program, the workshop organizers tried to dictate what would be taught and how the Art Ensemble of Chicago would present itself (!). It was "radical extremes," Joseph says. "It hasn't always been so nice [as it was at CMS]."

*Famoudou
Don Moye,
New Year's
Intensive,
1978-1979.*

PART II

9

The Golden Years

"We all see what's happening, and it's not that interesting. . . . We need it [CMS] now more than ever."

—Roscoe Mitchell

The Oehler's years, particularly 1978 through 1981, were the zenith of the Creative Music Studio's evolution. Some have called these the golden years of CMS. In addition to the many guiding artists who had returned year after year and contributed so much to the Studio's growth, there were several fantastic artists who made their first appearances at CMS during 1978.

Collin Walcott, the classically trained percussionist, who was with the group Oregon until his tragic death in an automobile accident; Artie Traum, the guitarist who is known primarily in folk music, yet is also well known for his instructional guitar books; Nana Vasconcelos, the brilliant Brazilian percussionist who taught America what a berimbau is and became a steadfast supporter of CMS's mission, and of whom Jack DeJohnette said, "He has more rhythm in his little finger than most of us have in our whole body."

Ed Sanders, poet and founder of the Fugs, and Allen Ginsberg, the beat poet whose name has become practically synonymous with the so-called counter-culture, presented their own special blends of music and words that summer. CMS was, in fact, the venue for the premiere of Sanders' "Karen Silkwood Cantata," a multimedia presentation of poetry, dance, and music performed by CMS students.

Allen Ginsberg brought cellist Arthur Russell with him for his week of residency. He says, "Since I didn't know music, except homemade, I brought him [Russell] along to mediate between me and the trained musicians. . . . [I was] a little anxious that I wasn't up to the musical standards. . . . There were all those great, professional musicians."

William Blake's "Songs of Innocence," and "Songs of Experience" were the focus of Ginsberg's workshops. Russell's role was to teach the musicians melodies that Ginsberg had come up with to go along with his recitations of Blake's poetry. Once all had become familiar with the melodic and metric structure, they were able to freely improvise together. This was something that Ginsberg had been working with since the 1960s when he had recorded the Blake pieces with Don Cherry, Elvin Jones, Julius Watkins, and other jazz musicians.

"I think some of the musicians may have gotten more familiar with Blake and enjoyed that," Ginsberg remembers. "Karl Berger and Ingrid put up with it. . . . It was unusual, it was puzzling because I didn't know more than two chords, anyway, four maybe. . . . This was a relatively innocent, coherent strangeness."

The 1978 lineup also featured Jerome Cooper, drummer with (at that time) the Revolutionary Ensemble; Grachan Moncur III, the trombonist who appeared on so many "progressive" jazz albums of the late sixties; Trilok Gurtu, the Indian tabla player and multipercussionist, whom *Down Beat* magazine named number-one percussionist of 1994 in its critics poll; Marion Brown, the saxophonist; Jeanne Lee, poet and "free-jazz" vocalist; Andrea Centazzo, the Italian percussionist, who is little known in the States, but made a big impression at CMS; George Lewis, trombonist, composer, and alumnus of Chicago's Association for the Advancement of Creative Musicians; Nick Brignola, the baritone saxophonist whose ambition, according to Leonard Feather in *The Encyclopedia of Jazz* , was to become one of the "top five baritone saxophonists in jazz" and whose grandfather played tuba with John Philip Sousa; and Ryo Kawasaki, the Japanese guitarist who gained attention in the States in Elvin Jones's band.

Good Press

An article in *The New York Times* in January was the first of a number of important media pieces to appear in 1978. It recounted a Carnegie Hall concert, which featured Leo Smith and his group New Dalta Ahkri, Oliver Lake, Karl Berger, and pianists Ursula Oppens and Amina Claudine Myers. The writer's opinion was that "conceptually, [the concert] . . . had much to recommend it ."[1]

---

1. Kenneth Terry, "Jazz and Classical Musicians Interact at Woodstock," *The New York Times*, July 23, 1978, p. 15

Allen Ginsberg, Oehler's Mt. Lodge, 1978.

Janet Grice and Mark Ralston, Oehler's Mt. Lodge, 1978 or 1979.

Regardless, he seems to feel that as the performers "tread the elusive borderlines between 'jazz,' classical avant garde and ethnic music" they "approach the exuberance of jazz" in only the final piece of the performance. It was not exactly a glowing review, but it did get a mention of CMS into the Times, which is always a public relations coup.

Later in the year, *The Times* published another article, which highlighted CMS's series of outdoor, summer concerts. The focus of the piece was the series' blending of "avant-garde classical music" and "innovative jazz." It places CMS's activities in the larger context of the history of jazz and classical musics' unions, citing the Association for the Advancement of Creative Musicians, Gunther Schuller, John Coltrane, Garrett List, Stravinsky, John Cage, Karl Berger, Ornette Coleman, and others.

The magazine *Apartment Life*, in its July issue, pitches CMS to college students as an alternative to "a stuffy classroom."[2] The article would seem to be tailor-made to draw the merely curious—the type of student who would frustrate some of the seasoned players who were already disappointed at the level of musicianship of many of the students. It lumped CMS sessions into the magazine's category of "vacations with a purpose." Nonetheless, the article was one of very few that didn't appear in a music journal or in the music section of a newspaper. It was (and is) good to spread the word as far and wide as possible.

Jazz Magazine ran a piece in its fall issue called "Where Teaching Meets Jamming,"[3] which did a good job of relating the value of the informal, unplanned musical interactions (the "jamming") that ignite as a result of so many creative musicians gathering under one roof or out on the lawn.

Nana and Trilok

In fact, an informal unplanned musical interaction is the only way to describe the first meeting of the percussion monsters Nana Vasconcelos and Trilok Gurtu. Nana told me that he and Trilok (who were both introduced to CMS by Don Cherry) knew each other's reputation, but before CMS had never met. The summer of 1978 was the first that

---

2. Leslie Stackel, "Trips for the Real Trouper," *Apartment Life*, July 1978, p. 14.

3. Mark Plakias, "Where Teaching Meets Jamming," *Jazz Magazine*, vol. 3, no. 1 (fall 1978), p. 28.

either had come to CMS and for Trilok, at least, the first time in the United States. When Nana first arrived at CMS, even before he took his things to his room, he asked, "Where's Trilok?" Someone explained that Trilok was down at the pool, learning how to swim.[2] Nana decided to wait. He still hadn't been to his room, but, as always, he had his berimbau with him, and he sat down and started to play.

Soon, Trilok came by with a wet towel around his head. He saw Nana and went to his room and got his tabla and came back. "We don't say hi or nothing," says Nana, "just sit and start playing."
Language barrier? No problem. Music is the language.

The Return of Carlos Santana

On August 26, the CMS grounds were the venue for a concert that anywhere else might have seemed somewhat unusual. Nine years after Carlos Santana helped to make Woodstock a household word with his band's stinging performance at the festival, and five years after he devoted himself to the spiritual teachings of Sri Chinmoy, he returned for a very different show. This time, at CMS, it was actually Sri Chinmoy's concert, and Santana joined him and his group Sri Chinmoy Rainbow as guitarist and arranger. In an article in Kingston, New York's *Daily Freeman*, Santana was quoted as saying, "I'm fortunate enough to be able to reach two masses now. It's a great opportunity to touch and reach people."

"Santana, whose spiritual name is Devadip, though he is still known as Santana by most of his fans, said 'everything about the Woodstock festival came back to me as we drove up here on the thruway today. I remembered the dynamism of the people that weekend. It was something. . . . Today we have a beautiful day. The weather is fine, the music will be fine, and there will be good feelings. I'm glad that can't be commercialized.'"[4]

---

3. Whether or not Trilok ever learned to swim didn't emerge from my conversation with Nana. But I found out later from Jim Quinlan that Trilok did learn to drive on that trip.
4. Rick Remsnyder, "Carlos Santana: Everything is Now Clear," *The Daily Freeman*, August 31, 1978, p. 27.

The Musicmobile

Early in 1978, the fund raisers of the Creative Music Foundation, primarily Marianne Boggs and those who were assisting her, pulled off what was probably their finest achievement. This was during Jimmy Carter's presidency, before Reaganomics had reduced the government's largesse to a downward trickle. CETA (Comprehensive Employment and Training Act) grants were available to fund local economies in the hope of bringing more people into the workforce, without creating a federal bureaucracy to do so. The Creative Music Foundation was able to get ahold of one of these grants, which was good for about $400,000. With this money, the foundation created the Musicmobile.

No, it wasn't actually a truck or bus that went out into the community to distribute music, in the way that a public library's bookmobile distributes books. It was an outreach program that brought a widely appealing variety of ensembles into senior-citizen homes, mental institutions, prisons, schools, and other facilities in the Hudson Valley region that might not otherwise have had any live music to offer.

These were not your typical gigs, however. There was the time, for example, when The Suspenders, the Musicmobile's jazz-rock outfit, played a Halloween party at the Hudson River Psychiatric Center's macro- and microencephalitic ward. Tom Collins recalls that "that was Donnie Davis's first gig. He didn't put his saxophone in his mouth the whole night. He just stood there with his mouth open." On other occasions CMS's Musicmobile would feature "Take Me Out to the Ballgame" singalongs at senior-citizen homes, a string quartet at a park in Kingston, New York—duos, trios, large groups—whatever the situation called for. Michael Garden, a percussionist from Detroit, who also was the Musicmobile cook, remembers that the Musicmobile audiences were the most receptive, appreciative, and enthusiastic audiences that he's ever played for. By all accounts it was a huge success. CMS benefited and the community benefited.

The Musicmobile musicians were twenty-three of the Studio's most talented and dedicated associates. All had begun at CMS as student participants, but had remained with the Studio in whatever way they could devise. Several were living and paying rent at the Studio. They had all devoted themselves to living their music, and CMS offered the most creative, nurturing environment that existed.

One member of the Musicmobile's woodwind quintet would have been remembered for the instrument she played, if nothing else. Janet Grice, in addition to being the only bassoonist to attend CMS, was also one of the best trained, most disciplined students to attend. She was another of the many who had gained solid, classical training at the New England Conservatory in Boston. Her discipline was due, in part, to her study of Kundalini yoga, which she began teaching at CMS shortly after she arrived.

One night I overheard Joseph Jarman speaking on the phone to a friend of his in Chicago, another improvising bassoonist. It seemed that he had called him up just to sing the praises of this young white girl who could really play. Several other leading musicians took notice of her, and Janet eventually performed or recorded with Anthony Braxton, Julius Hemphill, Leroy Jenkins, George Lewis, Anthony Davis, Butch Morris, Nana Vasconcelos, Don Cherry, and others. In the middle eighties, she spent a few years in Brazil on a Fulbright scholarship, playing, researching, and making the most of the connections she had established with CMS's strong contingent of Brazilian musicians.

The CETA funds gave the Musicmobile musicians financial backing that allowed them to remain in Woodstock and to develop their music, while maintaining an association with CMS and its unique assemblage of some of the finest musicians in the world. The terms of the grant dictated that all of the Musicmobile employees be present at CMS every day and that they practice or perform for eight hours every day!

Being paid to practice was like a dream come true. It's an extremely rare situation for any but the most commercially successful, mainstream, musical organizations. CETA monitors would show up from time to time, to ensure that CETA employees were carrying out the tasks that they were being paid to perform.

Marianne Boggs was the only person involved who was not paid by CETA. "My role," she says, "was fiscal oversight as well as making sure that these people got to the gigs and weren't stoned and remembered to bring their instruments. . . . I had to do all of that and oversee CMS. . . . We really were running a huge organization—more than a half-million-dollar organization, annually—out of those bizarre half-bedrooms over at Oehler's lodge!"

The Musicmobile project brought a sense of constancy and cohesion to the Studio. Creative confusion, sometimes bordering on anarchy, had been the more typical watchword for CMS regulars. Cohesion and constancy were new, hopeful, energizing descriptors.

The financial backing for individuals wasn't much, a little over minimum wage. Its importance lay in boosting the morale and giving a sense of purpose to those involved. For Karl, this constancy meant that he would have a steady pool of talent for developing his Music Universe Orchestra. All of the Musicmobile musicians were well acquainted with

Karl's concepts and compositions; some, like James "Snake" Harvey and Donnie Davis, had been with Karl since the earliest days of CMS. And they were all there every day. It was the first time, actually, that Karl had been able to work out Music Universe concepts with a large ensemble over an extended period of time.

Unfortunately, the Musicmobile had a short life. By the summer of 1979, the CETA funds had dried up, and the project ground to a halt. The economic and political climate in America was changing. The Musicmobile's halt was a harbinger of times to come that would not support artistic endeavors that ran primarily on idealism.

Julie Haines on a Musicmobile gig, 1979.

10

Woodstock Workshop

"Improvisational music is an oral tradition, and so it works better when the actual performing artists are the ones who are educating. Because, a lot of times, what's imparted to a younger musician is something that sometimes can be formalized and other times just has to do with a way of living or looking at the world or a creative stance. It's not so much about technique or technical matters. Just being around and living together in those situations and having the actual, active artists come through there—and they're not full-time teachers, but they're just there—is the key. . . . Everybody has their own story and their own way of dealing with [creative improvisation]. So, when you have a variety, a range of artists coming through who are enlightened to these things, the way that they express it, one [artist] might touch one student, and another might touch another."

—Adam Rudolph

The Creative Music Foundation began publishing its own quarterly journal in March of 1979, entitled *Outlook: The Creative Music Quarterly*. The tabloid-sized newspaper was born with great hopes that it would play a vital role in worldwide promotion of the Studio, and in disseminating information relevant to creative musicians and their listeners. Its mission was put forth in the masthead:

> "The Creative Music Quarterly is a unique journal in that it is written primarily by the professional musician. It serves as an informative source for audiences and musicians providing information on developing or-

ganizations supporting contemporary music, and most importantly as an outlet for the theoretical and philosophical written work that so frequently accompanies the musical output of the creative artist. In addition, career development, funding possibilities, and examination of current movements will be regularly featured in this publication."

The journal had revenue-raising potential, too. Anything that spread CMS news more widely had a chance of reaching even more funders. And advertising helped: Journals like *Coda, Jazz Magazine, Cadence, Ear,* and *Musician* and record companies small and smaller, such as ECM, Hat Hut, and Corn Pride all bought space in *Outlook*.

Had the journal continued, it would have stood as one of the richest source of interviews and writings from the minds of people who were setting the pace in contemporary creative music and art.

An interview with Dave Holland gives young musicians invaluable information on how to practice and how (and why) to listen. Byard Lancaster discusses the "hidden steps in the master's plan" in a stirring, poetic essay on the jazz musician's place, role, and function in society ("My concept (1980s) is to work harder than hard."). The poetic investigator Ed Sanders delves into the effects that metric patterns of words can have on our psyches and on our musculoskeletal systems, and he encourages us to develop and internalize our own "psychologically ornate set of personalized metrics." Drummers Charles Perry and Jack DeJohnette break down some of the mysteries and complexities of "meter against meter"—odd and seemingly incongruous rhythmic groupings within a four-four context. And the programs, artists, schedules, hopes, and dreams of the Creative Music Studio are recorded in the writings of Karl Berger, Jim Quinlan, Marianne Boggs, and others.

Unfortunately, though, *Outlook* only lived through a handful of issues in 1979 and 1980. Sue Pilla, a flutist who came to CMS from Ann Arbor, Michigan, and who ended up as coordinator for *Outlook*, told me that the publication was doomed from the start. It, too became a victim of the CETA cuts. Even if it had been funded, the turnover of people who were interested in and capable of putting out a quality journal four times a year was so great that it would likely have folded anyway.

Garry Kvistad and Woodstock Percussion

One of the artists who arrived at CMS just in time to be featured in *Outlook* before it folded was percussionist and instrument builder Garry Kvistad. Garry moved in 1979 from the Midwest to a house in West Hurley just a few miles from CMS. He knew of the Creative Music Studio and the Woodstock area's history and reputation as fertile ground for artists. He was well schooled in contemporary, experimental, classical music and had been performing a piece by Frederic Rzewski with the Black Earth Percussion Group, which he had started while teaching at Northern Illinois University and the University of Cincinnati's College Conservatory of Music.

"When I first got here I looked into CMS and found out that, first of all, they were doing some great concerts. So I'd go to these concerts, and I started meeting different people. Karl asked me at some point within the first year or so if I would teach a class. That's how I got connected there. It was a great experience; and to top it off, I was able to ride my bicycle there.

"What was going on there was that people were teaching what they liked to teach, rather than what they had to teach. That was the beauty of it. People would come in, and if they had been working on something that was a little off the beaten track, they could present it to the students there, and the students would take it or leave it. . . .

"What I was just getting into was tuning and instrument building and listening a lot deeper to things like overtones and spectrum of sound and that. What I tried to work with the students on was the combination of pitch and rhythm, the way those two things interact. Because the kinds of rhythms that I was interested in were a lot of polyrhythms. And I realized that's what's happening with intervals—that there's these intense polyrhythms happening. And the simpler, the more pure the tuning system was, the easier those polyrhythms were. So there was a direct analogy between music that is very accessible, that had very simple rhythms but very well grounded rhythms; [they are] actually analogous to tuning systems such as just intonation and more pure tuning systems.

"I had my students play and learn from easy to complicated multiple rhythms, simultaneous rhythms, and also I would talk to them about the overtone structure and a little bit about the physics of sound. That's what I found fun, rather than just teaching percussionists technique and stuff like that. They kind of came there with an understanding that they would learn a lot of that stuff on their own or elsewhere."

Garry's contribution was distinctive because his interest in making instruments had led him to augment his music education with instruction in acoustical physics, metallurgy, and woodworking. He began to acquire his own equipment and build wind chimes while still in Cincinnati.

After moving to the Woodstock area he began to branch out, making different kinds of instruments for professional percussionists. With his background in the acoustics of metal and wood, he also became adept at tuning marimbas and xylophones. His enterprise grew to the point where he needed to hire help; and in the CMS student body he found an eager labor pool. It was a fine arrangement, for a time. Garry was generating an income for himself, and he was able to employ CMS musicians, allowing them to bring in a little cash.

However, "it didn't take long to realize," says Garry, "that musicians really didn't want to work in a factory, because that's basically what it was—production work. Even though a lot of them made good use of that money, if they had a gig, that came first, and I understood that."

Although, his CMS labor pool did eventually dwindle, Garry never lacked qualified help. At about the time when CMS dissolved (late 1983 to mid 1984), his Woodstock Percussion, Inc. began to receive substantial enough demands on production that he was able to attract local people who were interested in instrument building as a vocation. Today, the company is a thriving operation, supplying professional musicians and just plain folks who appreciate finely crafted, expertly tuned wind chimes and other makers of beautiful sounds.

Percussion Intensive

The last session that I attended at CMS happened to be the Studio's first Percussion Intensive—one week in May 1979, devoted entirely to drummers and percussionists. It was a chance for me to become reacquainted with masters Jack DeJohnette, Ed Blackwell, and Don Moye and to meet for the first time the brilliant Collin Walcott (who at the time was still with the group Oregon) and the inimitable Nana Vasconcelos. This group of guiding artists would have had sufficient drawing power for me regardless of circumstances; but it was spring, and spring meant the end of cabin fever at CMS; it meant a rejuvenation of spirit; and it meant playing outdoors, where the drums were really meant to be heard.

In America, the opportunity for drummers to congregate, play, study, and share knowledge collectively is a rarity. There are organized drum and bugle corps. And there are informal jam sessions in the parks of most major cities. Disciplined study groups in which drummers and percussionists can explore and internalize rhythms of America, Africa, South America, and India, on the other hand, are practically unheard of.

In Detroit I was fortunate enough to take part in Roy Brooks' Aboriginal Percussion Choir, an aggregation modeled after the group M'Boom, of which Roy is a charter member and Max Roach is the founder. And I have visited a drummer's teaching collective in Harlem, taught by Charlie Persip and other pros. In most cases, though, instruction in the drums in America and Europe takes place in private lessons, or is handed down through families as in Latin, Puerto Rican, and Cuban communities.

At this intensive session, trap drummers worked with and attempted to absorb the artistry of Jack DeJohnette, Don Moye, and Ed Blackwell. We explored jazz techniques primarily. Jack was fire and drive. Ed was tonality and fluidity. Moye's watchword was focus. There was hand drumming, too. I still don't know where all the conga drums came from, but we had groups of ten or more playing African rhythms with Moye, Brazilian rhythms with Nana, and whatever Collin Walcott had in his trick-bag of 'round-the-world rhythmatisms.

Collin had been trained in Indian music on the tabla and sitar, but also had an education in strict, academic, classical percussion. He told us how, at the university, he had practiced the triangle up to eight hours a day! Nana gave us all a chance to struggle with the berimbau, and stressed the importance of vocalizing rhythms. He did things with his voice and tongue that we had no hope of emulating. The sounds and syllables that one employs in giving voice to rhythms, he explained, will be determined by one's native language. We tried it and found that certain syllables that a native speaker of English is more comfortable with worked to create the same rhythms that he was voicing using his native Portugese.

The entire session was a banquet of rhythm and rhythm instruments of every description. Not a sound was made, however, without the intention of expressing the highest caliber of musicality. Too often percussionists and their instruments are regarded more as noise makers than skillful and creative contributors to a musical composition's full realization.

From this session I carry one of the most vivid, enduring, and fond memories of all my CMS experiences. At the end of Ed Blackwell's part in the intensive, Marianne Boggs came around to ask who might be able to drive Ed to his home in Middletown, Connecticut. There were two factors that placed me in the front running for this job: I wanted to spend as much time with this man as I possibly could, and I had a new car—not mine, actually, but a family-owned 1978 Oldsmobile Cutlass. So I set off on the trip with Ed Blackwell and two other drummers I'd invited to come along.

As I remember, it was about two-and-a-half or three hours to his home. Ed appreciated riding home in a new car, and he asked about my drive out from Detroit. I told him that I had made the twelve-hour trip without stopping, except to pee and eat. "You can do that 'cause you're a young man," he said.

All the way we talked about drums, music, life, his early days in New Orleans, the grief that the city put him through for marrying a white woman (he later received the key to the city), and his days with Ray Charles and Ornette Coleman. Any question we came up with he answered graciously. Ed Blackwell was one of the most generous, peaceful, gentle souls ever to play music.

When we arrived at his home, Ed invited us all in. As we visited, he showed us some notebooks of drumset exercises, which he had devised and which he was perfectly willing to let us copy. We were like kids in a candy store. We grabbed our pencils and scribbled like crazy for a half hour or so while Ed continued to enchant us with tales from the heart of jazz. I still have those exercises and still pull them out from time to time to work on some Blackwell ideas. These are treasured memories.

Ed Blackwell died in 1993, and I doubt that there's anyone who knew him who doesn't miss him. He'd had serious health problems for years, and was restricted by his need to be near kidney dialysis machines. Karl calls him a "genius" and more: "The guy was amazing. Blackwell alone would have been worth it coming to New York to live.

"I had the opportunity to record with him about three, four months before he died. It was one of the last records he made. He was such an amazing person because, despite being so sick—he was sick for many years, like, not having any kidneys—I think it was his music that kept him going. He became like a medical miracle. They wrote articles about him. I think the music kept him happening.

"I remember that [recording] session: He could hardly get to the drums. And once he was sitting there he was playing like an eighteen-year-old boy—this transforming energy. And then he could hardly get off the drums. You'd have to help him to get back to his seat. This man was a miracle. And we really miss him a lot, because there's really nobody working with that kind of concept. He was absolutely one of a kind. He never got, really, the honors of it all."

Karl regards this as a factor of karma. "People have different

*Ed Blackwell,
Woodstock Jazz
Festival, 1981.*

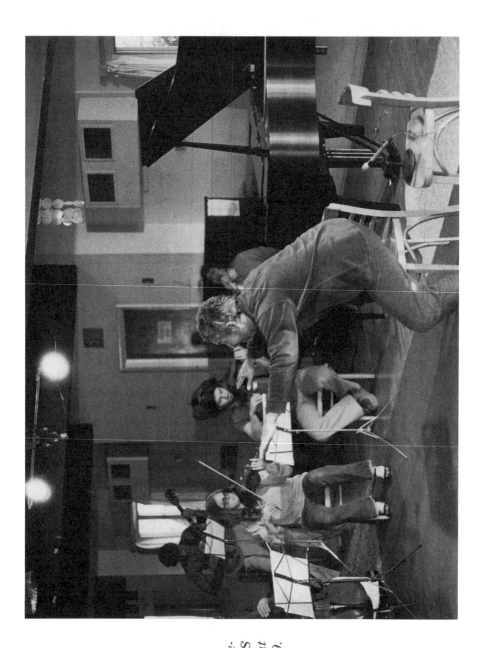

*Karl Berger re-
hearsing a CMS
orchestra at
Oehler's, 1979.*

karma. It's nothing you can explain from just one lifetime. People come into this life and they're already carrying a load of all kinds. And some are on the trail of going this way, and others are on the trail of going that way. You just put in the best you can. Also, he got on drugs very early. When I came to New York he was a drug addict. And after both kidneys failed, he had to, of course, stop taking drugs.

"He became a different person. You could almost say like a zen master. When he would sit down on the drums, it was a meditation. It was like four people playing—independence. The independence of it was, like, gruesome. There was not one note that you would play with him that he would not catch. He would catch all these notes and just throw them back. He was not just playing with you; he was getting all of your notes and throwing them right back at you.

"We did a couple of concerts together, which I won't forget. One of them was unbelievable. There was a Berlin festival called the Metamusik Festival. It was not a jazz festival. They were into some kind of world-music idea, but sort of a fancy festival with lots of money. So, they invited Blackwell and me to come, and they said what do you want as a setup? So I told them to have every kind of keyboard mallet instrument and any kind of drums that they know of on stage in any order. We arrived and there was hardly any room on the stage to move. It was filled with instruments. They had tympani—everything. So the concert consisted of us walking around playing all these instruments. We were just walking around, playing all this stuff for about an hour. It was so beautiful. Blackwell was a genius; and he died penniless."

Composers' Colloquium

Garrett List, trombonist and composer who had been working with Karl since the first days at the Turtle Bay Music School, organized two Composers' Colloquiums, one in 1978 and one in 1979. There was also a third colloquium in 1980, after Garrett moved to Belgium.

In informal, give-and-take, question-and-answer discussions among the composers and an audience of CMS patrons and students, some of the leading composers in America, in what might most readily be called new music, came together to discuss the state of music and composition at the time. One was broadcast over National Public Radio. Another (or perhaps it was the same one. It was difficult to glean a solid agreement from the memories of those involved.) was written up in the October 1979 issue of *Down Beat*.[1]

---

1. Arnold Jay Smith, "Reaching for the Cosmos: A Composers' Colloquium," *Down Beat* , October 1979, p. 19.

It had been Garrett's role, along with Karl, to create many of the CMS programs and to entice musicians to come to teach. After graduating from Juilliard in 1969, Garrett took on New York as a professional for every situation. His classical training and his interest in jazz and improvisational forms gave him the agility to move from Broadway shows, to salsa bands, to symphony orchestras, to jazz gigs, to commercial recordings—whatever was out there. He became a part of the scene in which classical musicians and jazz musicians were experimenting with overlapping concepts. This is where Garrett made his association with Frederic Rzewski, Richard Teitelbaum, and the group Musica Elettronica Viva (MEV).

They used to experiment in an aggregation they called the Space Orchestra, which would gather in the Space for Creative Development in a loft on West 26th Street. Garrett recalls: "Every Thursday we had what MEV used to call free soup. These things were just big improvisations;; anybody could come and play. We did this every Thursday afternoon for quite a while. . . . That's where I met Rhys Chatham for the first time and Jim Burton and guys like that; Julius Eastman I met there for the first time. It was, I guess Frederic [Rzewski], who, with Rhys Chatham, sort of organized the sessions. That was before The Kitchen really existed, on Broom Street. It was the first place where The Kitchen people started playing together.

"I'm sure I played with Karl there. He asked me to do some workshops on composing and improvising at the Turtle Bay school in Manhattan around '71 or '72. And that's the first time that I actually did any of that kind of teaching."

Garrett went on to become the music director for The Kitchen (in 1974, 1975, and 1976), one of New York's best known and longest-lasting "alternative" performance and exhibit spaces. He made a decision then to give up his free-lancing and perform only the music that he and his friends were creating. "It was a lean time," says Garrett, "but it was beautiful."

These friends happened to be some of the most influential improvisers, classicists, and experimentalists on the changing American music scene in the early and middle seventies. He had met most of them on the New York loft scene, at The Kitchen, and in his role as CMS program director. For him to create the Composers' Colloquium, then, was a natural outgrowth of his activities to that point. "It was part of my job as [CMS] program director. All these characters were there, and we'd had concerts where we mixed up their music a lot, already. Sometimes we had concerts where we had written music, and sometimes we had concerts where we had improvised music." These "characters" included Ken McIntyre, Michael Mantler, Michael Gibbs, John Cage, Maryanne Amacher, Frederic Rzewski, Karl Berger, Christian Wolff, Carla Bley, and, of course, Garrett List.

This coming together (the Composers' Colloquium and the workshops and concerts at CMS) of these people was, in Garrett's words, "a mix, but it was very consistent at the same time. There was a lot of common stuff going down between most of the people, in spite of everything. I guess that the idea was that we didn't see these musics as being so separated, and that they really did exist in sort of the same world, and they were jumping out of the same kind of background, in spite of what people would like to think.

"Cage was a student of Henry Cowell, and Cowell was, in spite of the experimental thing that he had, kind of an Americana boy. That's just my feeling about it. And Cage was sort of the same thing. He's, like they say over here [in Europe], 'an American original,' like Levi's or something. . . . What brings these people together is a basic feeling about the culture, what the American culture is and what is its fabric and how it's made up."

Garrett makes a clear distinction, however, between the work of those in the Composers' Colloquium and those in what he calls "the university American music scene." The composers who came together at CMS were part of a guild, so to speak, of American composers who are "actually going around and playing the music—much more concrete. You write it and you do it. All those people were like that. . . . It's sort of like reality oriented in that way about the actual performing of the music, but also in the fact that somehow or other there's some kind of a function of music in the society. And it's not just about expressing your own personal ideas, but that somehow there's a larger context for your work. Which is sort of an American attitude, in a way."

The third Composers' Colloquium took place over August 16 and 17 in 1980 and comprised a mix of composers that was quite different from the previous year's colloquium. Karl took part again, as did Maryanne Amacher. This year's panel also had a strong representation from the Association for the Advancement of Creative Musicians: Douglas Ewart, Muhal Richard Abrams, and George Lewis. Others participating for the first time were Michael Byron, Linda Fisher, Marvin Minsky, Jill Krosen, Julius Eastman, and Richard Teitelbaum.

AACM in Residence

The connection between CMS and Chicago's Association for the Advancement of Creative Musicians (AACM) was an inevitability, given Anthony Braxton and Jack DeJohnette's settling in Woodstock and their work with both organizations. It was this connection that made possible the New Year's Intensives with the Art Ensemble of Chicago and which provided Roscoe Mitchell the opportunity, in the summer of 1979, to put on a session constructed entirely to his specifications.

A *Woodstock Times* article from August of 1979 alluded to the significance of the mighty representation of the Chicago force in Woodstock:

> "When [Joseph] Jarman arrives in Ulster County this week to perform two concerts, four of the most influential creative musicians in the history of great black music will be in our own backyard. Roscoe Mitchell, who's been playing with Jarman since 1961 . . . is directing a five-week session at the Creative Music Studio. Drummer Jack DeJohnette and saxophonist-composer Anthony Braxton are two AACM members who call this area home. DeJohnette, Mitchell and Jarman go back to AACM-founder Muhal Richard Abrams' Experimental Band in 1963; when the Art Ensemble [of Chicago] went to France in 1969, Braxton followed the lead and went over shortly thereafter. Finding these four individuals in the same neighborhood independent of a pre-arranged AACM festival or one of those four-day AACM radio orgies Ivy League colleges have been sponsoring recently is a marvelous twist of fate. . . ."[2]

Roscoe, for his CMS summer session, chose and brought in the guiding artists and organized the workshops; he was, basically, in charge. The program that he constructed was the closest that many musicians in attendance would ever come to experiencing the intensity and depth of commitment that characterize the learning environment of the AACM. Whereas the New Year's Intensives with the Art Ensemble of Chicago had emphasized performance and the development of skills on various

---

2. Mitchell Feldman, "Joseph Jarman: The Complete Performer," *Woodstock Times*, August 2, 1979, p. 31.

instruments, this was a chance to look more in depth at some of the most innovative compositional structures ever to evolve from the "ancient-to-the-future" traditions of "Great Black Music." In addition to Roscoe's, there were workshops led by AACM associates Anthony Braxton, Leo Smith, Joseph Jarman, and the young up-and-comers trombonist George Lewis and guitarist A. Spencer Barefield.

Although the middle-to-late seventies was perhaps the most vibrant period for the AACM, these CMS workshops, important as they were, were tinged by an unfortunate, yet all too familiar, irony. The group of participants (students) was predominantly, if not entirely, white. "That was our biggest complaint," says A. Spencer Barefield. "We thought it was a wonderful idea. . . . But, we felt that, here we were, teaching black music, and we never had any black students. This is the way America works."

Barefield, a Detroiter, met Roscoe and the other members of the Art Ensemble of Chicago while he was a student at Michigan -State University, and the group was living and performing in the Lansing, Michigan, area. There has traditionally been a strong connection between Detroit and Chicago creative musicians, and it was only natural that Barefield, who at the time had already developed his own approach to playing the guitar and to compositional structures, would fall under the AACM's sphere of influence.

George Lewis, who was introduced to Karl, CMS, and the Woodstock scene through Anthony Braxton, was such a good fit at CMS that he was able to assume the position of program director in the summer of 1980. He put together a session that he entitled "The Composer/Performer Today," which was to be, according to a Lewis quote in *Outlook*, "one of the most challenging, wide-ranging summer programs offered anywhere."

He added that "the session will feature both week-long residencies by exceptional guiding composers and frequent full-day seminars in electronic music and new instrumental technique. The format seeks to broaden the student's experience with a wide variety of approaches to composition, improvisation, and performance. Special seminars in the business of music are also planned, as well as programs in dance, poetry, and video."

George brought in Anthony Davis, Douglas Ewart, and Richard Teitelbaum as composers in residence and had this to say about each:

> "Mr. Davis' thoughtful, detailed approach to the composition/improvisation interface has led him toward compositions combining periodic and nonperiodic repetition

with a kind of collective orchestration that has resulted in instrumental music of great beauty and expressive depth.

Mr. Ewart wears many hats—composer, woodwind player, percussionist, instrument maker, and craftsman. . . . The current chairman of the Association for the Advancement of Creative Musicians, Mr. Ewart presents works which embrace with authority several traditions at once; often simple in appearance, his music draws upon the entire body of world music for its inspiration. His extraordinary command of the woodwind family has been heard on records by Henry Threadgill, Anthony Braxton, Roscoe Mitchell, and George Lewis. . . .

Perhaps the leading exponent of the art of improvisation with the voltage-controlled synthesizer, Mr. Teitelbaum performs regularly with his beautiful-sounding Moog instrument, which was built by Robert Moog himself. As cofounder of the highly influential Musica Elettronica Viva (MEV), Mr. Teitelbaum helped to reshape the relationship of electronics to live instrumentalists."[3]

Woodstock Workshop Orchestra in Europe

In November of 1979, Karl took the Woodstock Workshop Orchestra on a four-week tour of Europe. Looking back on all that was accomplished at CMS, a tour of Europe by a representative ensemble of CMS guiding artists and senior students wouldn't be unexpected and might not seem all that remarkable. However, today, to propose taking twenty or twenty-five musicians to Europe for an extended stay, without backing from a major record company or corporate arts patron, would seem like a sheer fantasy.

The orchestra, itself, was something of a dream band: Karl, vibes and piano; Ingrid, voice and piano; Don Cherry, pocket trumpet and bamboo flute; Leroy Jenkins, violin; Tom Cora, cello; George Lewis, trombone; James "Snake" Harvey, trombone; Mark Ralston, oboe and English horn; Janet Grice, bassoon; Susan Veglia, French horn; Lee Konitz, alto saxophone; Oliver Lake, alto and soprano saxophones

---

3. George E. Lewis, "CMS Summer Programs 1980, Summer II—The Composer Performer Today," *Outlook: The Creative Music Quarterly,* vol. 2, no. 1, 1980.

Roscoe Mitchell, Oehler's Mt. Lodge, about 1979.

George Lewis,
Banff, 1980.

and flute; Donnie Davis, alto saxophone, flute, and clarinet; Tom Collins, tenor and soprano saxophones; Michael Lytle, clarinet; Terry Sines, bass; Trilok Gurtu, drums, tabla, and congas; Peter Apfelbaum, drums, percussion, and baritone saxophone. Even young Eva and Savia Berger were involved, Eva singing and playing piano and Savia on flute.

Don Davis recalls, "It was a gas. I got to sit in between Lee Konitz and Oliver Lake. As a young alto player, to be between Oliver Lake and Lee Konitz—that pretty much says it all."

One of the first stops on the tour was the Donaueschingen Contemporary Music Festival in Germany, where the orchestra was recorded live for an album on the MPS record label. All compositions on the recording are by Karl, except for one traditional Turkish tune. There was another recording made later in the tour, a bootleg Italian pressing of inferior recording quality, for which the orchestra received no money whatsoever. On the illegitimate one, however, "there's some really great playing; the group is a little bit more fiery," according to Peter Apfelbaum. "Those records were important if only for the fact that it was one of these rare times when Karl was able to really have his music played by a large group, which is one of the things that he always wanted to do. . . .

"[The tour] was a big moment for Karl—not that he hasn't had a lot of big moments in life, and he certainly had worked a lot; at that point he certainly was no spring chicken. But for Karl, it was an opportunity for him to work with a large band, which is something he really hasn't had on a consistent basis. . . ."

The tour went on to include other concerts in Germany, Austria, Switzerland, Belgium, Holland, Italy, and France. On one leg of the tour, the group discovered that while they were sleeping, the train that theyiwere riding had been split to form two trains, one of which went on to the band's next stop, the other on to points unknown. "Half the band arrived at this gig, without Karl," Peter recalls. "And we did a whole night of just spontaneous combinations of different things. James Harvey and I did a duet where I played piano and he played trombone. Oliver Lake did a duet with Trilok on tablas. It was just one of those things that happens due to circumstance, due to an accident. But things happen anyway—it was nice. People got together and made the show happen. Everybody could improvise, so there were all these different combinations."

The spirit and the spontaneity of the trip made it feel very much like being at CMS, but on the road. Students and teachers collaborated, performed, and grew together; the line that separated them was stretched to its limit, often losing its ability to mark a distinction. And there was the family atmosphere that was so typical of CMS events. Several of the musicians had brought their children along, and it was not uncommon for everyone to eat together or spend time together telling stories. I would say that it was much like a family vacation, except that a tour like that is, in reality, a lot of hard work.

11

Choirs of Angels

"Times are calling out for acoustic music, sincere music, nonmechanized music."

—Larry Chernicoff

The 1979-1980 New Year's Intensive was a "one-of-a-kind opportunity to examine the composition and organizational style and life philosophy of Cecil Taylor." So said then-program director Jim Quinlan in a quote appearing in a *Down Beat* article about the event.[1] Cecil and the Unit—Jimmy Lyons on alto saxophone, Jerome Cooper on drums, Alan Silva on bass and cello, and Ramsey Ameen on violin—brought in the new decade in a fashion that those who were in attendance have difficulty adequately describing. It was an experience every bit as mysterious as the music of Cecil Taylor would suggest that it might be.

During the workshop in which students met Cecil and members of the Unit for the first time, Cecil asked everyone to play something solo, so that he could get an idea of the range of musical personalities present. All of the students were nervous, but guitarist Joe Cohen remembers being nearly "paralyzed with fear."[2] Cecil said little or nothing after each player's offering. Robert Reigle, a saxophonist from Sherman Oaks, California, was thrown more than a little off guard when Cecil asked him, "What did you look like before you were born?"

---

1. Peter Rothbart, "Orchestrating the Collective Consciousness," *Down Beat*, April, 1980, p. 17.

2 . Joe Cohen, "Passing Over: Cecil Taylor and Memories of My Underdevelopment." *Hartford Advocate*, April 10, 1985, p. 25.

Robert hesitated just long enough so that Cecil moved on to hear the next player.

Lisle Ellis, a bass player originally from Canada, now living in the San Francisco area, experienced the mystery perhaps more intensely than anyone else during the session. Lisle had first come to the Creative Music Studio in 1975. From 1975 through 1979, he did a lot of traveling back and forth between Vancouver and Woodstock, taking Karl's philosophy (and sometimes Karl) back to the west coast, partly in the hope of shaking up some of the traditional musicians and music fans in Vancouver. In the process, Lisle set up a group called the New Workshop Orchestra, which was modeled on the AACM and continues as a viable force in the Vancouver creative music scene.

As Lisle got more involved in the music, however, and progressed as a player, he found himself becoming subject to a curious phenomenon. He was actually becoming more and more frustrated with music and losing more and more confidence, waiting for and expecting some level of satisfaction or at-homeness that would not come.

In late 1979, he was in Vancouver in a "ball of confusion." The 1979-1980 New Year's Intensive was the furthest thing from his mind. Paul Plimley, on the other hand, had heard of this upcoming session with Cecil Taylor and was fired up and determined to go.

Paul is a pianist and mallet-instrument player who had never been to CMS. He knew that Lisle had spent a good deal of time there and did his best to talk Lisle into coming along. With little enthusiasm and no expectations, Lisle relented and returned to CMS. Had he known what was in store for him, though, he probably would have been even more eager than Paul.

What Lisle had been dealing with was a frustration with the process of "demystifying the music," an expression that Karl often used. The methods of Karl's basic practice, which prescribe that music be broken down into its constituent elements, certainly do reduce the mystery of the music to something as simple as breathing and listening.

"It's all so beautiful," according to Lisle. "It's such an exquisitely simple concept, and it's very attractive. I was very taken with the concept, because it spelled some things out very simply. I threw myself into doing this practice very diligently; I worked very hard at it."

Lisle even began teaching basic practice in Vancouver. All the while, he had an itch that wasn't getting scratched. Something was missing; he inferred a promise that wasn't being fulfilled.

Enter Cecil Taylor and a totally different concept. Music, according to Cecil, is not something that we should be trying to demystify or divide and conquer. Rather than breaking down music, separating its parts, we should be working on music as a process of unification. Essentially, the message of leaving the mystery of the music alone was exactly what Lisle had been searching for. It's what relit his fire.

This is not to say, however, that these apparently opposing philosophies are working against each other. They do not cancel each other out. Music is a vast realm. An individual must navigate it with whatever tools he or she can best utilize. One cannot discount the idea that while two concepts might appear to be in opposition, they might actually be complementary. The music certainly can be simple and mysterious at the same time.

Lisle's account of a particular afternoon rehearsal session is a compelling example of just how mysterious a musical sojourn with Cecil Taylor can be. It was an occasion when the entire student orchestra was working on a piece of Cecil's music. "There was, like, forty seconds of music where this group hit. And, I don't know what it was, man, but the . . . orchestra was playing . . . and it sounded like somebody lifted the roof off the room, and a choir of a thousand angels came in and were singing hymns on top of the music. I don't know what happened. All I know is, it was this *incredible* feeling! I started to weep as I was playing the music. It was like a psalm that was so familiar. It was like coming home. And when I recount this to people, the hair starts to stand up on my skin. . . .

"That changed my life—that moment. Because I never knew that music could exist like that. I'd never heard anything like that, and I had never had that experience. I'd had exhilarating experiences playing music and been very moved, of course, by it, but never to that degree. I said to myself and other people, I don't know what that was, but whatever that was, that's what I want to dedicate my life to. . . .

"It was such a strange experience. It was only seconds long, and it felt like this incredible bubble was forming around the group, or, you know. . . it's impossible to really put this into words. I guess if we could we'd never play. And there was this feeling like it was going to do something, like it was going to go further than it had already gone. There was something ready to . . . the bubble was going to burst.

"And then the whole group stopped on a dime without any direction. And I'm talking twenty-plus players. Everybody stopped right on a dime, and we just stood there in silence and motionless. While this was going on, Cecil was standing next to me, and I could see him; he was laughing and throwing his head back and just, like, belly laughing. And as soon as it stopped, he immediately exited through a side door. Nobody could really say anything. Gradually they put their instruments down very softly. Cecil wouldn't talk about it. Even days later, he would never discuss that moment. He would never try to offer any kind of explanations or say, Oh yes, this is what you do; you just do this and this and this, and you get that. The mystery is that you never know."

I suppose that it's only fair, at this point, to recount how the "creative confusion" surrounding the public performances during Cecil's intensive moved one *Woodstock Times* writer to vent his anger and his condemnation of the CMS way of conducting business. His acrimony seems extreme, to me, but his comments do help to illustrate the fact that there was almost always someone who found CMS to be a little (or a lot) too loose and free in its operations.

The writer, Leslie Gerber, came to the New Year's eve concert with great anticipation of experiencing Cecil's "extreme virtuosity." He states, however, that he "should have known that CMS' usual bad management would spoil the experience." Although the concert was scheduled to begin at 9 p.m., it was nearly three hours later when Cecil actually sat down to play. There had been some warm-up performances by CMS students, but they hadn't been advertised and were clearly not what Gerber had come to hear. When Cecil finally did get down to business, however, Gerber got what he came for. He said, "He can play faster than the ear can hear, louder than the instrument should be able to respond to, and with more complexity than one mind should be able to handle, all at once. I sat frankly open-mouthed in astonishment as I saw him play passages that seemed well beyond the bounds of human capability. There is no substitute for seeing this phenomenon occur; I can't begin to explain or even describe it."

Despite the fact that the experience was "short-circuited by CMS' wretched presentation," Gerber was back the following week for another performance. This one was "billed as a recording session of music by Cecil Taylor performed by 'the CMS Student Orchestra and the Cecil Taylor Unit.'" According to Gerber, though, Cecil never played a note. Student groups performed; and groups of students performed in combination with members of the Unit. But no Cecil. "I don't think it would be an exaggeration to call this outright fraud and false advertising," Gerber claims. "My suspicions that the mis-billing was due to negligent incompetence rather than dishonesty don't make me feel any happier. . . . Thus the usual CMS sabotage continues. Obviously, whoever manages these concerts—if anyone—doesn't give a damn for the audiences, and I'll be extremely cautious before putting myself in CMS' hands again."[3]

3. Leslie Gerber, "Genius and Torture at CMS," *Woodstock Times*, January 10, 1980.

Banff

The tail end of 1980 found Karl and a select group of guiding artists providing instruction in a lofty atmosphere, as had the beginning of the year, but this time on a more earthly plane. The venue for this phase of the itinerant CMS was Banff, Alberta, in the Canadian Rockies. After nearly a year of negotiations, Michael Century, of the Banff Centre School of Fine Arts, was able to bring CMS to his part of the world. Michael Century, an administrator and a music educator, came to Banff at a time when there were big plans afoot to bring the Banff Centre from being a summer-only center to offering year-round arts training. His function was to plan these new activities.

He posed three options for augmenting the existing, two-week, summer jazz program, which was a run-of-the-mill, mainstream jazz workshop offering the experience of what is commonly called a band camp. The first option was to expand the mainstream, small-combo instruction; the second was to develop a large-ensemble/big-band program; and the third was, in Michael's words, "something that doesn't assume jazz at all," except as it fits into a broader context with classical and other types of music. As an example, he recommended the contributions that CMS was making, which he was aware of from people who had been there and from his own listening and reading.

This third option had enough appeal to Michael's boss that he was given the go-ahead to bring Karl and crew there for a three-week pilot program in December 1980, which was given the title "Advanced Studies in Improvisational Composition." The musicians who came were ostensibly representatives of jazz schooling (Karl, Ed Blackwell, Dave Holland, Jimmy Giuffre, Sam Rivers, and Lee Konitz) and the classical avant garde (Frederic Rzewski, Ursula Oppens, Pauline Oliveros—George Lewis, of course, would seem to be at home in both camps). The staunchly classical music department directors, however, were not in favor and actually "never encouraged anything related to jazz or any kind of nonclassical music. In fact," Michael goes on to say, "I had to set up a separate line of authority to do this. But it was always in conflict and against the wishes of some people."

The thirty students who were selected for the program were all accomplished professionals. They began their days with basic practice, attended classes and panel discussions held by the various CMS artists, and performed at night for the public. "The program was so intensive that people were exhausted. . . . It was a very, very rich program," says Michael. "[It] had a big impact, wildly successful—probably you could consider it one of the most high-impact programs done there. But it was strongly attacked and criticized by the classical department who found it a threat against their hegemony—which it very validly was. Here was a program—and I did this very deliberately—here was a program that was saying that the philosophy of CMS is very promising pedagogically because it proposes to train and produce artists who don't just do one thing, who actually do multiple things. And the examples that were given in that program were people who could play really high-level classical music, but who were open minded about improvising and moving in between the boundaries.

"The classical department didn't like that. They liked the idea that jazz music was something that was done as kind of a commercial thing within only a narrow stylistic band in what was considered sort of mainstream, sixties jazz. They had contempt for that, but that's what they wanted, because then they could treat it as a second-class program of marginal interest artistically. . . . They [could treat it] as a token thing that demonstrates the breadth of the overall department. They can say that the department does jazz, but of the type that they wanted to pick. This is why they didn't like the more broad-ranging approach.

"The pilot project was supposed to produce an experience. The idea was to test something that would then be used to implement a programmed thing. And of course, that was Karl's dream, because CMS never had any money, and here was this institution in Canada, which at the time had nothing but money, it had tons of money. It was the ideal relationship, whereby he could set up . . . CMS North, which he would run—an outpost of CMS—and have the same amount of, you could almost say, absolute control that he had at his own place. The major difference being that at Banff there was somebody there to pay the checks. That was how he saw the future. Now, it didn't really work out that way. First of all, the Banff Centre people over me, and also the music department [reached] no consensus whether there should be a permanent program or not."

CMS North, however, was not to be. Karl's vision and his desire to maintain the freedom that is so essential to his Music Universe concept would forever be in conflict with the powers that be in a classically oriented, academic situation such as the Banff Centre.

The next step for the future was something of a compromise between the "Advanced Studies in Improvisational Composition" and the accepted two-week, summer jazz program that had been in place. In the summer of 1981, Karl, Ed Blackwell, Lee Konitz, and Dave Holland returned for the "Banff Summer Jazz Workshop," which they conducted jointly with Canadians Big Miller (the late blues singer who had sung with Count Basie, Duke Ellington, and Jay McShann), Phil

Nimmons (who had taught in Banff's jazz program from the beginning) and trumpeter Kenny Wheeler (a Toronto native who has lived in London since 1952 and records for the European ECM label). Michael had taken the artistic elements of the CMS program, yet stripped away CMS. What was left was the best of the artistry of Karl, Dave, Ed, and Lee in a jazz setting that was less threatening to the Banff Centre's administration. Although the workshop was very successful, the future of the CMS influence on music at Banff was still very much in doubt. There was, in some respects, a tug-of-war between Karl and Phil Nimmons, each of whom wanted to run Banff's nonclassical (jazz) music program. The only sensible choice for Michael Century was, of course, Dave Holland.

"Dave kept alive a superb jazz program," Michael recalls. Through 1989, Dave directed what grew into a four-week seminar each summer, which was molded by a partnership between Dave and Michael. "We always kept saying, well, let's not just let it settle into the easy, doing jazz kind of program. . . . We always tried to have visiting composers who would stretch what's considered jazz."

They were able to maintain an approach that was pioneered with the 1980 CMS pilot program by bringing in, over the years, the likes of Anthony Braxton, Cecil Taylor, Muhal Richard Abrams, Roscoe Mitchell, George Lewis, and Anthony Davis. In 1987, however, Michael moved into an entirely new position in which his function was to set up a computer and media-arts center.

Dave's last year was 1989, and since that time all vestiges of CMS influence have vanished from the music instruction program. Fortunately, though, the whole pilot program was thoroughly documented in Michael's reports, and through written, photographic, and videotaped press coverage by Banff journalism students and local professional media.

Cecil Taylor, New Year's Intensive, 1979-80

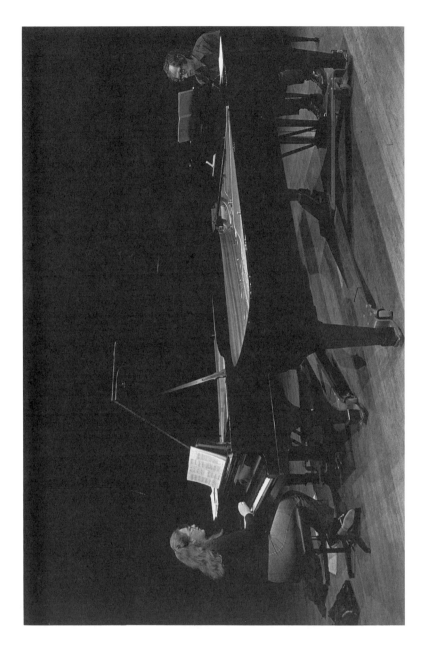

*Ursula Oppens
and Frederic
Rzewski, Banff,
1980.*

Lee Konitz,
Banff, 1980

12

Creative Financing

"Michael Jackson gets $10 million from Pepsi Cola, and he doesn't even touch the can or bottle. . . . Can you imagine what Karl could do with one-third of that?"

—Babatunde Olatunji

What is needed to develop, maintain, and grow an arts organization that is born of and nurtured by idealism? Where does all of the money come from that is needed to pay guiding artists of international stature to teach and perform and travel; to maintain facilities—mortgages, upkeep, taxes, utilities; to feed all who are a part of the organization; to purchase and maintain pianos, recording equipment; to entice hard-working people to contribute their time and energy to the cause; to promote the work through mass mailings, advertising, public-relations materials, artwork; to run a booking agency and record label; to take groups on tours of Canada, U.S.A., and Europe; and to take care of the myriad large and small expenses that pop up despite the best efforts to plan for all contingencies? It starts with a credit card—two, actually.

Karl recalls the Studio's inception: "We were living in a very small place, [paying] about $275 a month or even less. I started looking around for places where we could have the workshops. And I looked at this barn, and it was $500 a month—it was just too much. There were about five or six people looking at it while I was there; so, there was a lot of interest in it. I went home and said, 'No, we can't afford it.'

"The next day, the owner of the barn called me up and he said, 'Listen, I didn't like any of the people that were there, except you. I want you to be there. How can you do it?'

"I told him, 'Well, first of all, I can't pay you the first two months rent. Then, maybe I can pay you back what I owe you every month. But just to move, [we'd] have to spend money.' He said, 'no problem,' and we moved.

"The following two weeks, each week, a credit card arrived that I had applied for. Each had a $500 line of credit, so we used that to start the Studio. It was based on two credit cards. Amazing.

"I was inexperienced in business, but at the same time, I had an absolute drive about doing this. From the very beginning, we didn't have the money. But it always came from somewhere. It was miraculous, really. Whenever we needed some money, somebody, somewhere would come through with a thousand dollars or whatever."

Thus began *creative financing*. CMS administrators, who for a long time included only Karl, Ilene Marder, and whoever else could help out, were not business people. CMS was an artistic enterprise run by artists, who were making it all up as they went along. Their creativity and their determination to make it happen were the only tools they had to bring it to fruition. "We were very carefree about the development of CMS," says Karl. "If we would have sat down with an eighties mind to figure out whether this could be done, it would have never happened. It only happened because it was running on a seventies attitude. It ran on pure idealism, it didn't run on money."

Ilene and Karl spent many a late night working on grant applications, using principles of numerology to come up with amounts that would make the whole budget balance. Ilene recalls that it was "the most fun" that they had as administrators. Yet, despite their unorthodox methods, they became accomplished grant writers. Ilene figures that she and Karl were able to bring in over $90,000. They also developed relationships with several banks in the area. "I was in the back of every bank within a twenty-mile radius," Karl recalls. "I knew every president of every bank." These relationships proved to be lifesavers on a number of occasions.

New Year's Eve, 1979, was one such occasion. It was, in fact, an example of creative financing at its finest, an episode that Marianne Boggs calls the "loaves and fishes moment." Cecil Taylor, who along with his ensemble had been conducting the 1979-1980 New Year's Intensive session, made the pronouncement that if he did not have $10,000 cash in his hand before the beginning of his New Year's Eve concert, he would not perform.

Marianne had expected to pay him at the end of the session, still nearly a week away. The money would have been no problem. Both the session and the concert were sellouts. Cecil Taylor had drawn people every bit as well as had been expected. On the morning of New Year's Eve, however, the money was in foreign currency, checks, promissory notes—every form but U.S. cash. Fortunately, it was a week day, and the banks were open.

According to Marianne, "We went from having zero cash and very little reliable collateral at nine in the morning to having $10,000 in my hand by the time he [Cecil] needed it. . . . Bankers taught me how to kite checks. Bankers taught me how to [deposit] a certain kind of check at two o'clock, so that by three-thirty it was in there and you could take it out as cash. It was an amazing series of tricks that allowed us to function. . . . We kept that place alive by any means we needed. . . ."

Determination, idealism, and drive are not the whetstones upon which sound business acumen is honed. They can take an organization a long way, but, as with CMS, they often yield unorthodox business practices. They can also produce some resentment along the way. There were many supporters of creative music who could overlook or extend due dates for money owed, and many of the local businesses that supplied CMS stretched the organization's credit to the limit. However, bankers, landlords, and vendors of fuel and groceries are not in the music business and will only extend themselves so far. Not all of the musicians who came through could appreciate creative financing, either.

Musicians—students and guiding artists—are nearly unanimous in their praise of the artistic vision of the Studio and the value of the creative output. Nonetheless, there were some who came away with a bitter taste from the "looseness" of the operation. Some were offered wages that never materialized. Some, who came as students and remained as administrative supporters, eventually had to leave because of the futility in trying to scratch out a living in such an unpredictable financial environment.

Two factors created the financial hardships that in the end proved insurmountable. The first was the purchase of Oehler's Mountain Lodge. Karl acknowledges that the move got them in way over their heads financially.

In Karl's words: "That was really, in retrospect, what, in the long run, killed CMS. We went to a property like that too early. Because we were not in a financial position to have a place like that."

From the very beginning, when CMS was renting Oehler's and buying their food, it was a financial albatross. "We had absolutely no money in the bank, and we were supposed to come up with these kinds of amounts [the $1,500 to $2,000 a week that Oehler was asking] every week."

Ben Patterson, who had been expected to supply the type of

financial savvy that would carry CMS forward toward its goals, was the one who had brought about the Oehler's deal. Karl had been in Europe and expected to return to find a new home in the Mead's Mountain House. Oehler's was a complete surprise to him.

"[Patterson] ran into this Oehler's deal, and we followed him on that. That was my mistake, for which I paid until just recently. . . . I should have stopped him, but I was in dream state. . . . He was supposed to be this expert, but he turned out to have delusions of grandeur. . . . He wanted to build an empire . . ., but he moved too high too fast. . . . He told me that he had made an agreement with Oehler, and if we gave him [Oehler] $7,500 . . ., he would start this real complicated purchase-lease agreement. I said to Patterson, 'That's all well and good, but we don't even have seventy-five dollars in our bank account. What are you talking about?'"

As was the pattern for CMS, the money did come from somewhere—almost out of thin air. At that time, Karl and Ingrid had decided that their Witchtree Road home, because it was no longer being used as the Studio, had become too big for them. They began to look around and soon found a smaller house that was much more suited to their needs.

Karl asked the owner about the rent, and the owner asked him, "Why would you want to rent it if you can buy it?" Of course, Karl's only honest response could be, "I can't buy a house; I don't have any money." The owner, "a real slick kind of landlord type," told Karl, "I'll show you a way that you can do it."

His game was this: Borrow $2,500 from whomever would lend it, and pay that amount to him as a down payment on the house. He and Karl would then make an agreement and Karl could get a mortgage. Once Karl had the mortgage, he was to go to the bank and get a $10,000 construction loan, which at that time (1977) was very easy to get. Karl could then immediately pay back the $2,500 he had borrowed, and he would have $7,500 left over for other things.

Karl thought to himself, "Seven-five? I just heard that! Where was that figure coming up from? It was just a few hours earlier when Oehler had said we need seven-five to get into the lodge!" So that's exactly what Karl did. He borrowed the money, bought the house, and took the $7,500 to put down on Oehler's Mountain Lodge.

Although Karl can laugh at the remembrance of these shenanigans, he readily admits that "it was absolutely irresponsible. . . . And the whole CMS went that way financially, the whole time. . . . Always, miraculously, some money would come from somewhere. . . ."

The second factor that led to CMS's financial collapse was the change in the political and economic climate as Ronald Reagan took over the presidency from Jimmy Carter.

"Basically, what killed CMS was Reaganomics," Karl says matter-of-factly. "If I had at that time known what I know now, we would have closed the doors the moment Reagan became president."

The biggest blow that CMS took from Reaganomics was the discontinuance of CETA funds. With no CETA funds, there was no longer a Musicmobile. This was not only a financial hardship. Having the steady support that CETA provided had been a real morale booster for the Studio. Without those funds, without the Musicmobile, morale flagged, and some found it no longer financially feasible to remain at CMS.

There was also the crucial matter of the U.S. dollar's value relative to foreign currency. By 1980, over 50 percent of the student body was composed of musicians from Europe, South America, Canada, or Japan. The rise in the value of the dollar made it simply unaffordable for many international students to attend. Furthermore, by 1982, CMS was no longer able to issue student visas. It became impossible to maintain enrollment at a level that finances required.

Times were hard. Money was tight. Through the seventies, there had been enough sixties-flavor tolerance left over to allow an undertaking such as CMS to grow and flourish, nourished by only creativity, risk-taking, and idealism. In the eighties, however, the essential fuel was capital; and those with the capital saw no payoff coming from an arts group born of a sixties spirit of freedom of expression.

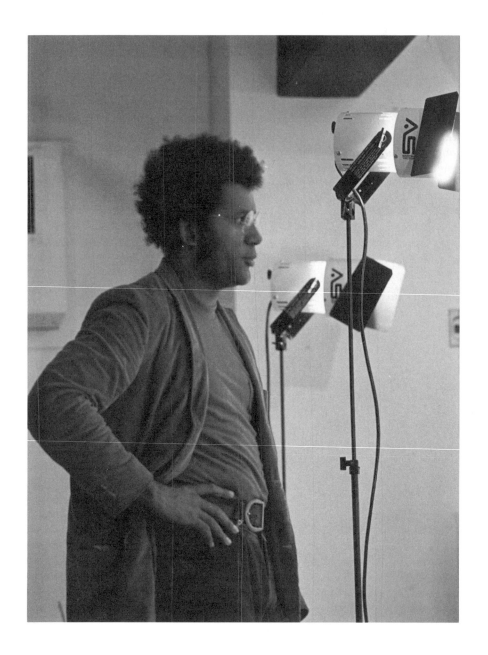

Anthony Braxton, Oehler's Mt. Lodge, about 1979.

13

World Music

"If you think of what happened in the late sixties, you have, musically, a situation where jazz and the classical avant garde were closing ranks. In other words, the real avant-garde players in jazz were breaking free from the rules. And the whole thing about the sixties was that: breaking the barriers and cutting through all kinds of stuff. So it was a very revolutionary kind of approach. And I was in the middle of all of that at the time. One of the things that was leading to my giving workshops and studying and so on was to find out what now? . . . What's next? What can we do with all these pieces that we just broke apart? I realized that what needed to be done was for everyone to personally decide: What do you want to do? And to develop disciplines. And so for me it was how do we develop disciplines that are not just guided by stylistic considerations? . . . As we progressed, I naturally got to meet all kinds of people from different parts of the world, and the world-music thing started to get stronger and stronger. . . . So, basically, CMS developed along those lines. But there wasn't a plan like that. We were just improvising."

—Karl Berger

It seemed to be a fundamental irony in CMS's maturity that as the financial picture began to look more and more bleak, the music and the total outpouring of creativity took on an ever brighter gleam. Some consider the world-music sessions to be the most exciting and enlightening offerings in the Studio's history. They were summertime affairs, the first of which was held in 1979, the last in 1983.

It was inevitable, given Karl's Music Universe philosophy, that CMS would eventually attract musicians from all parts of the globe. It was natural, too, considering the Studio's genesis in the free-jazz movement. Jazz has always absorbed musical influences from around the world, at the same time that it has been changing the musical

121

outlooks of musicians in Europe, South America, India, Africa, and elsewhere. To teach musicians to find their own sounds, to go beyond traditions and deal with universal elements, it would be necessary to explore the differences and similarities between jazz, European classical music, and the forms of myriad ethnic groups.

Karl talked about this philosophy in one of our conversations in 1994: "If you play a chord on the piano, and I play the same chord on the piano, it will be a completely different sound. If you become aware of that, you can cultivate your sound; you can get your own sound. . . . No other person in the class will have the same sound. But you'll only become aware of that once you're aware of the strings moving. So first you have to do the tuning exercises to hear that. Once you hear that, you become very attuned to sound in a very new way. So, if you bring that together with your awareness of the rhythm, then you have a whole body to work with that has nothing to do with any particular tradition. . . . It's worldwide musical sensitivity.

"Then you can go to India and play with somebody, and you don't have to worry about traditions. You can just start getting a feel for whether this person is someone I can play with. World music is just like getting married. You have to be compatible; you can't play with everybody. There's no system that makes it possible to go to anybody and just play. That's why a lot of world-music production is nonsense; because the producers are putting musicians together, and sometimes it works, and sometimes it doesn't. It's just like if you would throw together men and women and say, OK, you guys get married. . . .

When we [Karl and Senegalese talking drummer Aiyb Dieng] play together, it's like he was my other self, like we were soul brothers. We just play, no problem. Everything was wonderful—smooth. Then I went to Senegal, and I met other guys playing the same stuff, and it was not the same feeling. It had nothing to do with the music; it had to do with the affinity of the personalities. And that is a worldwide phenomenon. It's not like you, in Ann Arbor, might find someone better to play with than in Africa. It has nothing to do with that. It has to do with affinities of personalities, and they are worldwide. They are not national, or whatever; it has nothing to do with age. You just find certain people that you can play with. And the more advanced you get in your playing and hearing, the more selective you'll become with that. But on the other side, the results will [get] equally better."

Indian Music

Karl and Ingrid had been drawn to Indian music since before CMS began. While at Naropa Institute in 1975, they made a connection with G.S. Sachdev, a bansuri flutist and master of North Indian classical music, who was on Naropa's staff. Through Sachdev, CMS developed associations with several other Indian musicians, which grew into a tradition of Indian influence at CMS. Ilene Marder, who was also on the Naropa trip, began studying flute with Sachdev. Her personal connection with him, combined with her administrative function with the Studio, more or less ensured that there would be a strong Indian input in Woodstock. Terms of the grants that Ilene had secured from the New York State Council on the Arts stipulated that CMS present a certain number of concerts in Woodstock and around New York state. This enabled her to book several concerts with Sachdev and other Indian musicians.

One of these was sarod player Vasant Rai, who died during the eighties. He and G.S. Sachdev both belong to the lineage of Indian musicians who had studied with Allaudin Khan, considered to be one of the all-time great Indian musicians. Vasant Rai had also studied with Ravi Shankar, perhaps India's best known sitarist and also a disciple of Allaudin Khan. Vocalist Lakshmi Shankar, a relative of Ravi Shankar, and violinist L. Subramaniam also performed in concerts booked by Ilene. Sachdev often performed with tabla player Zakir Hussain, son of Alla Rakha Khan, *the* tabla player of the day. Zakir Hussain had also worked with John McLaughlin. Ilene describes him as "a real rock and roller," a young guy who was into "cross-cultural things . . . and a master, master tabla player." K. Paramjyoti, who was a chemical engineer by profession, was another tabla player who worked with Sachdev, Vasant Rai, and many Indian musicians who came to the States.

Although these musicians were on hand in 1974 and 1975 for performances sponsored by CMS, it was primarily G. S. Sachdev and vocalist Pandit Pran Nath who taught regular sessions as guiding artists.

Don Cherry and Jim Quinlan

Don Cherry had also studied music in India. However, he blended his teaching of Indian forms and rhythms with all of the other influences he had garnered from his world travels. It was his own unique gift.

He was not only an extraordinary teacher, imparting his own knowledge of music, amassed through a long career as a performer and absorber of musical traditions around the world; he was also something of a world-music, human-resources agent. Wherever he went, Don forged relationships with the most influential musicians. He was the first American contact for several musicians who ended up coming to CMS to teach and who, in many cases, found other opportunities to teach, perform, and record as a result of their CMS associations.

From the beginning, it was Don Cherry who opened up the musical channels from Woodstock to Africa, India, South America, Turkey, the Caribbean, and the Orient. He was the epitome of the world musician; his roots were in American jazz, but he branched out and absorbed influences from the entire planet.

Allen Ginsberg revealed another side of Don Cherry to me that I had been unfamiliar with: "He [Don] acted as a major actor in an opera I did with Robert Wilson in Hamburg about four or five years ago. He was one of the main figures there, both acting and playing. He was marvelous as a mime/pantomime, high-stepping silhouette. . . . His whole body was full of music."

The manuscript for this book was nearing completion in October of 1995 when I got the news that Don Cherry had died. I knew that his health had been failing, but that he might die never even crossed my mind. It had been a comfort to know that someone was out there, traveling the Earth, bringing back to us not only the knowledge of the world's traditions in improvised music, but some of the world's finest improvisers as well.

Karl Berger had envisioned Don as a "great elder" in a new incarnation of CMS. Now he's gone and it becomes starkly apparent that nobody else could ever have the same vision and energy to catalyze a lifetime of travel, study, and performance into a singular world-music force.

Nana Vasconcelos says that Don Cherry was "a school in himself." And that he was. For Nana, knowing that he is the only remaining member of the unique and influential trio Codona must have a profound effect. First Collin Walcott was lost in a tragic auto accident and now Don Cherry has died of illness— both gone much too soon. "There will never be another Codona," Nana laments.

Nor will there ever be another Ed Blackwell, John Cage, Stu Martin, David Izenson, Ismet Siral, Jimmy Lyons, or Julius Hemphill. It seems too soon that the list of departed guiding artists should have grown so long.

It is a strange task to have to go back over a manuscript and change all references of an individual to past tense. In a sense, though, it didn't really seem necessary. Don Cherry lives on in his music.

Don Cherry in an outdoor workshop at Oehler's, about 1980.

*Collin Walcott,
Woodstock Jazz
Festival, 1981.*

What he began was a celebration of the unity of the world's peoples; and the message spreads through the language of music, which transcends all cultural boundaries.

This celebration is growing. It's infectious. It's changing the tone and rhythm of everything we hear in music. Listen to movie soundtracks. Listen to pop songs on the radio. Look at the programs of high-brow musical societies. Listen to the improvisers. And always remember Don Cherry as a pioneer.

Jim Quinlan credits Don Cherry with opening the doors to world music for him, directing him to the people who would make the Summer World Music Festivals[1] of 1979, 1980, and 1981 so successful. Jim first came to CMS from Ann Arbor, Michigan, in 1975, when the Studio was in Mt. Tremper. His intention was to study bass with Dave Holland.

He soon returned to Ann Arbor, though. In 1976 and early 1977 he continued the broadcasting that he had been doing at WEMU, a National Public Radio affiliate station at Eastern Michigan University. He also began booking concerts. One of the first, if not the first, that he booked was at Eastern Michigan University and featured the group Oregon, Don Cherry, and Leon Thomas. It was arranged through the CMS booking agency of the time. From the playing that Oregon and Don ended up doing together that night came the Collin Walcott and Don Cherry collaboration that would later manifest as Codona, with Nana Vasconcelos. Don and Jim also "cemented a very nice relationship," according to Jim, from their working together on that concert. As a matter of fact, Jim had put Don up at his own home in Michigan.

Jim returned to CMS in the summer of 1977 as an intern. This time, he came not as a musician, but as a budding administrator and booker of talent for concerts and workshops. He went back to Eastern Michigan University to get a B. A. in arts administration, and when he returned to CMS in 1978, he quickly became, at twenty-three, the director of programs and services for the Studio. With Don Cherry's guidance, Jim created the first full-fledged Summer World Music Festival in 1979, and from then on, world music became the centerpiece of CMS's musical banquet.

---

1. These summer sessions were in different years called *sessions, festivals,* or *seminars.* All three had the same, basic, performing and learning environment.

Summer World Music Seminars

For five weeks that summer, CMS students were served up even more Indian fare by Trilok Gurtu and Steve Gorn, American-born expert in Indian, Indonesian, and Asian music, whose specialty is the north Indian classical (bansuri) flute. Steve became a mainstay at CMS, an important teacher at the world-music sessions until the end.

From Africa came Alhaji Bai Konte and his son Dembo Konte. Alhaji Bai Konte was, according to Jim, "one of the most revered kora players of the twentieth century . . . the undisputed master of the kora at that moment. . . . When he passed, it was a big time of mourning in the African music community."

He spoke very little, but "was one of these inspired people that just resonates and radiates this kind of wisdom, knowledge, spirituality. He was very heavy." Percussionist, song writer, and group leader Ahmadu Jarr, from Sierra Leone, was, contrarily, a very verbal and animated teacher. Having been based in Sweden, he was accustomed to teaching African music and culture outside of Africa. "He was probably one of the most popular of all the African teachers," says Jim. Foday Musa Suso, a kora player from Gambia who came to the States as a member of the Mandingo Griot Society, came that summer and participated in subsequent world-music sessions in 1981, 1982, and 1983.

Nana Vasconcelos and Guilherme Franco, Brazilian percussionists, were there. Franco, who had been working for some years with McCoy Tyner, came to CMS at the invitation of Trilok Gurtu. Franco's approach was to put the collective CMS ensemble "through a series of rigorous percussion classes based on salsa themes and some compositions recorded by Miles Davis."[2] Nana had, by this time, become established at CMS as a rhythmic life-force and remained a very welcome presence throughout the Studio's remaining years.

Don Cherry's travels had also taken him to Turkey, where he discovered Ismet Siral, Murat Verdi, and the brothers Faruk and Haci Tekbilek. These musicians, particularly Ismet Siral, became some of the most talked about of all the international musicians who came to CMS. "That whole Turkish thing was very much an advanced kind of view in terms of world music," according to Jim Quinlan. "Still, it's not very well acknowledged. It's such an interesting crossroads . . . between

---

2. Mitchell Feldman, "Nana Vasconcelos at CMS," *Woodstock Times* July 19, 1979.

Alhaji Bai Konte, Oehler's Mt. Lodge, 1980.

Ismet Siral,
Steve Gorn,
Trilok Gurtu,
Ingrid Sertso,
Nana Vasconce-
los, Karl Berger
(left to right),
Woodstock, New
York, about
1980.

Asia, Europe, and Africa. And musically, you've got such a deep absorption of those influences that, I think, there's something very fundamental to what they're doing there. It opens up your ears, also, to the whole Arabic sound. . . . It's the kind of music that makes that other sound accessible. That's one of the great things that the Tekbilek brothers and Ismet [did that] really, really had a big influence."

This was not like some ethnic fair, where the different groups present their distinct cultural artifacts from separate, isolated stations. Music has a way of uniting cultures and nationalities, such that all who attended these sessions were able to come together for a continuous sharing of information and creative ideas. There was a synergy that resulted from all of this blending that made this and subsequent world-music sessions unique. And it wasn't just in the class settings; people were together day and night, playing, teaching, learning, living the music. It was a celebration.

Nana describes the exchange of ideas that took place as "incredible . . . unique." Where else in the world might you find master Brazilian, Turkish, and Indian musicians sitting down to play together—and having it work? The rapport between Nana, Trilok, Ismet Siral, and Murat Verdi was fantastic. The four of them played day and night, in and out of workshops, as what they jokingly called the Baklava Jazz Club.

Many of the same artists returned for the 1980 Summer World Music Session. They were joined by Jerry Gonzalez (Cuba), Yaya Diallo and Aiyb Dieng (Africa), Barbara Benary and Iris Brooks (Indonesian music), Z.M. Dagar (India), Erasto Vasconcelos (Brazil), and the Mandingo Griot Society.

Adam Rudolph

Adam Rudolph, one of the founding members of the Mandingo Griot Society, remembers that summer (1980) and the following summer as a "tremendous experience." This is from a guy whose whole musical upbringing has been a tremendous experience.

Adam grew up in Hyde Park, Illinois, a suburb of Chicago. Now, all of us are influenced by the musicians closest to us, those neighbors and members of the community who are more experienced and are also willing to pass on their knowledge. It just so happened that the musicians in Adam's neighborhood were the founders and the movers of the Association for the Advancement of Creative Musicians: Fred Anderson, Henry Threadgill, Muhal Richard Abrams, Steve McCall, the Art Ensemble of Chicago, and others.

Adam actually started out learning hand drums from George Favors, the brother of Malachi Favors of the Art Ensemble. "I used to hear them [the Art Ensemble of Chicago] all the time," Adam relates. "They used to come and do workshops at my high school. I'd go hear them when they first came back from Europe. Man, there'd only be twenty or thirty people there; and they'd give these incredible concerts, like three, four hours long."

And then there was the blues. The legendary Muddy Waters and Howlin' Wolf also lived in the neighborhood. "What's so funny," Adam goes on, "is [that] growing up in that neighborhood . . . you don't think that [that] music is anything historical or special or unusual. It's just the music that's goin' on around the neighborhood. It wasn't 'til I left that I realized I had been there at a really special time in a special place, and that kind of thing isn't going on all the time everywhere."

After finishing Oberlin College in 1977, Adam traveled to Ghana to study the drums more in depth. There, he met Foday Musa Suso, who was his neighbor in a compound of houses at the Institute for African Studies. Together they decided to form the Mandingo Griot Society, and they returned to Hyde Park, where Foday Suso still lives. "We called Hamid Drake, who's an old, old, friend—we had been playing together with Fred Anderson, who's one of the founders of the AACM—and we got a bass player and started playing. . . .

"This was before any sort of world beat, African music at all. . . . And nobody was really doing anything with the traditional instruments. We had kora, electric bass, drumset, and percussion."

Their first record, which Adam produced, was on the Chicago-based Flying Fish label. "Having been a fan of Don Cherry's," Adam says, "I called him, we got a hold of him, and invited him to come play on the album. So he came and played on the first Mandingo Griot Society album. That was kind of how we plugged into the whole world of meeting Karl, and Collin Walcott, and Don's associates."

Adam saw a greatly expanded view of that whole world when, in 1978, he and Hamid went to live with Don in his house in Sweden. It was an environment that Adam recalls was much like what he later experienced at CMS, but much less formal. "It was out in the woods, and all kinds of musicians were coming through. We were playing music twenty-four hours a day. Trilok Gurtu came through and Ahmadu Jarr and The Everyman Band. . . . It was an incredible experience. . . .

"A lot of us recognize how important Don is . . ., but he's under-acknowledged as far as the whole growth of this idea of world music. He's a great artist." Adam's respect for Don Cherry is echoed over and

*Adam
Rudolph and
a student
group, outside
at Oehler's,
1980 or 1981.*

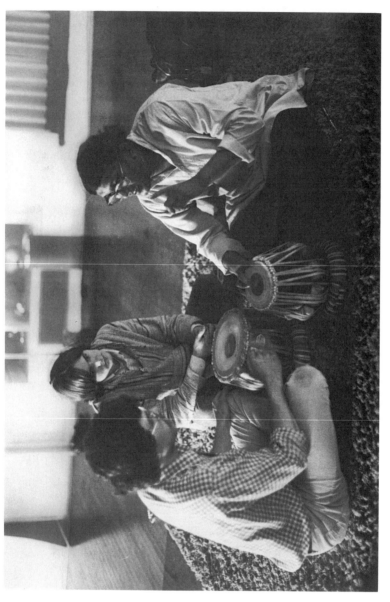

K. Paramjyoti (right) and students, Oehler's Mt. Lodge, about 1980.

over by so many musicians. Even rock groups like the Talking Heads attribute their forays into world music to Don Cherry's influence.

Don was responsible for establishing CMS's Turkish connection, meeting and bringing over Ismet Siral, Murat Verdi, Haci Tekbilek, and Faruk Tekbilek—fantastic musicians whose magic had a strong hold on anyone attending these world-music sessions.

When Adam and Hamid met Ismet Siral and Haci Tekbilek at CMS in 1980, an instant bond was formed. The four would play together around the clock, developing Turkish Sufi music and African Mandingo music together. They were not hindered by schedules or locale. It was summer; they could play indoors or out. Their only responsibilities were to share the music and transfer the benefits of their experience. During the day Adam and the Mandingos taught hand drums, polyrhythms, and the Mandingo style of music that they had brought back from Africa. The Turkish musicians taught Turkish music. Rhythm training was provided for all instrumentalists. At night, after dinner, the four would begin playing together and go until midnight or one o'clock. They would then take a break and repair to the kitchen, whereupon Hamid Drake would make chai tea.

"We'd call him 'chai baba,' because he was so great at making chai tea," Adam recalls. After the first night, a couple students heard them in the kitchen and came down to investigate. So, Hamid made a bigger pot of chai. Each night, a few more people would come in for this midnight chai break, and the pot kept getting bigger and bigger. "After a few weeks, the whole school—I mean everybody was there—would come down at midnight or one in the morning, and Hamid would make this giant vat of chai."

Eventually, Hamid found a chai-making disciple in a woman from Denmark, who took over as "chai baba," and the nightly gatherings continued. And the Sufi/Mandingo music continued, the players frequently greeting the sunrise. These were "magic moments," according to Adam. Bright moments.

Into the Community

The spirit of the world-music sessions and the musicians who participated was far too exuberant to be contained within the grounds of CMS. It had a spillover effect that enlivened the entire surrounding area. Nearly all of the performers who came to CMS to spread their music had opportunities to do concerts in and around Woodstock and Ulster County. And there were ample opportunities for the populace to come to CMS and listen, dance, and celebrate with the artists.

Several concerts took place at Woodstock's Kleinert Gallery. One, in December of 1979, featured G. S. Sachdev performing sunlight ragas on bansuri flute, accompanied by K. Paramjyoti on tablas. Marilyn Crispell and Ilene Marder provided the drone on tamboura and swarpeti, respectively.

One of the benefits that Ilene recalls from being both a student of and promoter for Sachdev was the chance to perform with him. "Whenever Sachdev played, I always played srudi-box [another name for the swar-peti]. Once I played tamboura, but I didn't like it, because I was on the other side of him, and I couldn't really hear him as well. [Playing the] srudi box, you're right between the flutist and the tabla; you're right in the middle. You hear them; you hear their breathing. It's like making love. It's very sensual."

In 1980, the Kleinert presented a series of Saturday night concerts to coincide with the Summer World Music Session. These featured Collin Walcott, Aiyb Dieng, Ismet Siral, Haci Tekbilek, Faruk Tekbilek, Gamelan Son of Lion (Javanese music), and others in various groupings.

World music fans who couldn't make these affairs could take in the world-music film series at CMS on Friday nights or the by-the-pool concerts on Sundays. All were welcome to come and swim, picnic, dance, and enjoy the summertime while listening to the sounds of Conjunto Libre (with Jerry Gonzalez), Grupo Colobo, the Mandingo Griot Society, The Everyman Band, and others on different Sunday afternoons.

In October, CMS offered a Brazilian Samba Dance Party with Guilherme Franco and his ten-member samba band. Later in October Foday Musa Suso treated the public to his kora playing and story telling in the Gambian tradition. Ahmadu Jarr showed his community spirit by performing solo and with the CMS World Music Orchestra at a benefit arts fair for the Woodstock Public Library in the summer of 1981.

There were concerts throughout the world-music sessions that were likely to present any combination of these international artists: Ed Blackwell with Trilok Gurtu; Trilok Gurtu with Aiyb Dieng; Ismet Siral with Steve Gorn and Badal Roy; Nana Vasconcelos with anybody and everybody; Andrea Centazzo or Ahmadu Jarr or Abdullah Ibrahim in solo concerts.

World-music summers were a time for reggae music, too. The first reggae festival, the Sun Energy Festival, was held September 2, 1979. In addition to the music of Jah Malla with Max Romeo and Woodstock's own Marc Black, the festival, a Public Arts and Recreation

Trilok Gurtu (left) and Aiyb Dieng, outside at Oehler's, 1980 or 1981.

Nana Vasconcelos, Oehler's Mt. Lodge, about 1978.

Center (PARC) event, featured solar-energy exhibits, arts and crafts, and food concessions. It was considered a significant enough event to rate a notice in *The New York Times*.[3]

The second festival, held August 31, 1980, presented Jah Rushalem, The Core, Moja Nya, and Black Uhuru and drew over 1,000 people. In 1981, the groups Black Sheep, Moja Nya, and Sons of Creation were the acts on hand for the Labor Day Reggae Festival. There was also plenty of West Indian food, "healthful beverages," beer, and, as always, dancing.

Olatunji

CMS presented a smaller affair in July of 1982, a "reggae dance party," which again featured Black Sheep and Sons of Creation, and a group called Itiopia. This time, Black Sheep was augmented by the esteemed presence of Babatunde Olatunji, the Nigerian, who after moving to the United States in 1950 and graduating from Atlanta's Morehouse College in 1954, turned America and the rest of the world on to African drumming with his now-classic "Drums of Passion," recorded in 1959.

When I first heard "Drums of Passion," it was 1973; I thought that it was something new. When Olatunji told me in 1994 that it had been out for thirty-five years, I was flabbergasted!

It's not clear exactly when Olatunji began to teach at CMS, but soon after July of 1982, he began an association with Karl and Ingrid and CMS that continued until the close of the Studio, and included a tour of Senegal, Zaire, Gabon, Nigeria, and Ghana in 1983. Others in that touring ensemble were Aiyb Dieng, Trilok Gurtu, Steve Gorn, Nana Vasconcelos, Ingrid, bassist Mike Richmond, and pianist George Schutz. "It was a fantastic cultural exchange," says Olatunji.

At CMS, Olatunji did what he has been doing all over North America for decades and continues to do at his center in Harlem.[4] "What I was doing there was actually to support what Duke Ellington said about jazz, in a way, that jazz is a phenomenon that has evolved from so many sources, and Africa's contribution to jazz is rhythm.

---

3. Harold Faber, *The New York Times,* Friday, August 31, 1979 ("Weekend" section).

4. Olatunji's earlier studio was forced to close due to financial hardship. He had been teaching drumming, dancing, and culture there for $2.00 a ninety-minute lesson. This center was where John Coltrane gave his final performance in 1967. The admission price was $3.00.

"So I was teaching people how to play the drums—and then the polyrhythmic nature of African music—connected with the language, and the dance. I tried to show that all three go together; it's a total theater. You never see a complete [African] stage presentation without singing, dancing, and drumming. All of that is put together to tell a story, to educate, and remind people of what has transpired before. . . .

"So, people come to my class. They learn not only how to play the drums, they will learn how to dance to the beat of the drum, and they will learn how to chant. One of those things will have to get you to want to be in the class. Once you get in there, you will see how all three are connected. And then I put it together [to show] that, look, there is a cultural basis for our unity. So whether you come from Germany, England, or Australia, there is something about your society that is so common to where I came from. . . .

"We start with what we call body percussion—clapping of the hands, stomping of the feet. How did we entertain ourselves before instruments were made? We go through that history in my presentation before we even come to the drums. Then we experiment with people who play saxophone, flute, oboe. . . . And then we put the whole thing together and see how we can come up with a composition, and then put a program together at the end of the week. So, for a whole week or two, people eat, talk, sleep, hear, and drink about culture. The environment was such that you can't help but learn something while you're there.

"I would love to see CMS come back again, because it's unique in the sense that it's geared toward putting musicians from different backgrounds, from different countries, together. I think we need that now, more than ever before."

Watazumido Doso Roshi

The concept of *music as not music* was presented in the fall of 1981 by Watazumido Doso Roshi, Japanese bamboo flute master. Doso Roshi stopped by CMS on a tour of U.S. universities and imparted a whole new way (for most) of regarding the discipline of self expression through sound. He is one of those rare people whom the Japanese government has designated a national treasure. He presents himself not as a musician (and certainly not an entertainer), but as one who is totally devoted to developing his life force by utilizing and strengthening his breath. The bamboo flute is simply a tool for that development.

For this reason, he shuns the highly polished, lacquered, and well tuned shakuhachi that is typically considered the Japanese bamboo flute. His is a much less processed instrument, which he creates from a piece of bamboo that is far closer to its natural state. You can even see the bamboo guts if you peer down the flute's shaft. The use of such a seemingly unplayable instrument demonstrates Doso Roshi's commitment to the discipline of the breath over the expression of melodies. In fact, he calls his instruments *suijo*, which translates as "concentrated breathing tool." For his purposes, the term *flute*—or the shakuhachi itself—is worthless.

"The way to find the place from which music comes is by developing the breath. The ordinary, mechanical breathing we do only suffices to keep the body alive, but nothing can be created from it. It is a weak breath. Even the rough breathing that work or exercise forces from the body is weak and of a little value. It is necessary to develop the strong breath, after which it is possible to breathe softly and without weakness. Music is secondary; the way of Watazumi is the strengthening and deepening of the life force and the breath. Since I must have some way of knowing how my breath is doing, I blow into a piece of bamboo and hear how it sounds."[5]

In a six-hour presentation, the seventy-one-year-old master told stories, talked of his way of life and his philosophy, played the bamboo flute, and demonstrated his daily exercise routine based on martial-arts movements. At that time, he had been performing these movements for 3,050 consecutive days. He was aiming for 3,500. It was obvious that his discipline was as much in line with the asceticism of martial-arts training as it was with the aesthetics of music-making. On a chilly, blustery October day, dressed only in shorts and running shoes, the master went through his routine using a long oak pole, perhaps seven or eight feet long and and inch and a half in diameter. Spectators huddled in their warm coats. Jack DeJohnette, Baikida Carroll, and others watched in heated comfort from their cars.

Although Dozo Roshi has rejected the Japanese government's national treasure designation, he asked that he be made an honorary professor of CMS, a position that was cheerfully created for him. His promise as he left was that when he returned to the United States, he would come only to CMS. Anyone who wanted to see him would have to visit him there.

---

5. From a paraphrase of Watazumi Dozo Roshi's words by Rafi Zabor in "Creative Music Studio," *Musician,* February 1982.

Tom Cora with homemade instruments, outside at Oehler's, late 1970s.

PART III

14

The Tenth Year

" . . . There clearly wasn't much finacial reward but there was obviously something going on that inspired people. This brought in a number of musicians who were really exploring with ways to integrate non-Western music into a jazz context. Practically everyone that has been significant in exploring in that direction passed through CMS, at some point or another."

—Steve Gorn

The artistic success that CMS had achieved by 1981 warranted that the Studio mark the close of its first decade with a celebration that would draw attention to itself from far and wide. In August of the tenth year, the first annual Woodstock Jazz Festival was held as a tenth anniversary celebration and a fund-raising event to help whittle down some $30,000 in debts incurred from general operating expenses and from the purchase of Oehler's Mountain Lodge. It was the high point of a year that also included an extraordinary percussion intensive with Ed Blackwell, Jack DeJohnette, Collin Walcott, Nana Vasconcelos, and Trilok Gurtu, and an incomparable, five-week World Music Seminar. Unfortunately, it was also the last annual Woodstock Jazz Festival, a fact that is perhaps symbolic of the point that CMS had come to. It was an unqualified artistic success that happened in spite of financial obstacles that were becoming staggering.

The festival was put into motion by Jack DeJohnette and Pat Metheny, who, along with Karl and the CMS booking crew, were able to assemble Chick Corea, Anthony Braxton, Nana Vasconcelos, Collin Walcott, Miroslav Vitous, Baikida Carroll, Dewey Redman, John Abercrombie, Aiyb Dieng, Ed Blackwell, Lee Konitz, Julius Hemphill, Howard Johnson, Marilyn Crispell, the Woodstock Workshop Orchestra, and others (including Jack and Pat). It was an extraordinary day of music, despite cold and rain. "With all this talent that we have, I guess we should have made it a two-day festival," Karl was quoted as saying in a *Woodstock Times* interview before the concert.[1]

One bleak note of the day, though, was the fact that Dave Holland, who had been scheduled to perform, became gravely ill and was hospitalized with an infection in a heart valve. There was a great deal of concern for Dave in the musical and artistic community and a fear that he would be unable to continue to perform. He did, however, recover and is going strong today.

With this level of creative activity still in full force after ten years, it must have seemed incomprehensible that anything could work strongly enough against the Studio to force it to close. Karl continued to infuse CMS with his optimism and idealistic zeal, and the ship remained afloat. In a "Goals and Visions" statement that he wrote in March of 1981, Karl acknowledged the financial hardships that been wrought by the Oehler's purchase, but refused to see these as omens of doom. Ever the visionary, he was actually looking to build a new property in Mt. Tremper.

> "I feel strongly that CMS not only needs a facility totally compatible to the needs of its programs, but also one that is not a towering fiscal burden dictating a seamless success story. As we are presently heading into a time of total political/economical unpredictability it is crazy for us to be burdened with a load of more than $150,000 of capital debts, tied into very rigid payment schedules with constant performance pressure. It makes me feel extremely uncomfortable. . . .
>
> My suggestion: We secure land in Mt. Tremper, create an architectural model of the facility we want and go for a major capital fundraising drive. . . .
>
> I [would] like to concentrate my efforts on this major (fundraising) goal of integrating CMS into the Mt. Tremper community and creating an environment conducive to long-term involvement of participants by making it a place one really wants to be; the place to be."

Oehler's was no longer the place to be, for a number of reasons beyond the fact that it was a "towering fiscal burden." Karl was con-

---

1. Eric Andersen. "The First Woodstock Jazz Festival: And a Conversation with Karl Berger." *Woodstock Times*, September 3, 1981, p. 44.

cerned because the rate of student turnover was so high. He concluded that the facilities were to blame, in large part, for the dissatisfaction that prevented students from making commitments to study at CMS over the long term. The accommodations were certainly not conducive to the nearly constant sound barrage of rehearsals and performances. They were designed, of course, as short-term housing, with no concern for any acoustical necessities, let alone those of a world-class, music-study enclave.

Isolation was also a detriment. Oehler's could have been in the middle of nowhere as far as those participants without cars were concerned, and that was most of them. There was no public transportation, and the closest store was three-and-a-half miles away. Being at the Studio for weeks on end in the winter could cause a very real cabin fever. It took an unusual monastic discipline to focus entirely on one's music for those long stretches of time.

The "Mt. Tremper community" that Karl referred to was a gathering of artistic and spiritual groups (particularly the Zen Arts Center, which had settled into the old Lutheran Camp) in the Mt. Tremper area. CMS had actually begun and influenced this movement with its early residence in the Lutheran Camp; it had become Karl's goal to bring CMS back "into the new Mt. Tremper community."

Although Mt. Tremper was in a location that was somewhat more mountainous and rural than the Oehler's spot, it had more to offer in the way of a general store, post office, restaurants, state parks, and access to public transportation to Woodstock and New York City.

In spite of any signs that the economic climate was becoming more foreboding, the musical outpouring from CMS continued. In fact, looking back at the number of concerts, events, and sessions offered, it's a wonder that the entire CMS crew didn't drop from exhaustion at the end of the year.

*Marilyn
Crispell,
Woodstock
Jazz Festival,
1981.*

15

Back to Mt. Tremper

"It [CMS] was really an exceptional situation. It was so relaxed, without all the rigamarole of academia."

—Richard Teitelbaum

"Why did CMS close?" Several people have asked me this, incredulous that a place of such creative spirit and artistic value would not just go on and on. No extensive analysis is required, really. It simply became financially unrealistic to continue; debts became overwhelming, and the nation's political and economic climates became even more unfavorable toward funding of the arts.

Late in 1981, after the Woodstock Jazz Festival (which had held so much promise for rejuvenation, but produced only a moderate financial return), both Marianne Boggs and Jim Quinlan left CMS. Marianne had maintained, up to this point, a crucial position as administrative trouble shooter and can-do, make-do Jill of all trades. Jim had essentially built the world-music program and proven himself to be, as program director, capable of putting together memorable and invaluable sessions.

Although their leaving might not have felt like such an upheaval at the time, because of the artistic momentum that the year had built up, it had to have taken some wind out of the Studio's sails. And looking back, it's easy to see it as a symbol of decline. Karl threw a Thanksgiving party to thank all of the people who had worked on the jazz festival and to say thanks and goodbye to Marianne and Jim.

Pauline Oliveros

New hope came, though, with the composer and performer Pauline Oliveros. Karl had known of Pauline's successes as the founder and one-time director of the Center for Music Experiment in San Diego, California, and had asked her to come and help redirect CMS's financial decline. Pauline had developed a relationship with the Rockefeller Foundation while in San Diego, and there was good reason to believe that she could attract their support for CMS.

In fact, "that would have happened, right in 1981," Karl laments. "I was at all the meetings; I knew what was going down. Pauline had the power, because she was very strongly related to that foundation through her previous work. . . . But it was too late. History went different ways."

"My skills were not really fund-raising skills," Pauline told me. "At the time, I think Karl was desperately looking for someone to help pull things out. But my participation didn't really help it."

It is possible, though, that no one's participation could have been strong enough to defend against the national economic forces of the time, which were anything but friendly toward the arts. According to Pauline, "the economics of the period were [such that] it [CMS's financial state] was not going to turn around. . . ." She reiterated the irony in the fact that, even though the Studio had been built up to include over 50 percent of its student body from outside the United States, these same people could no longer afford to come because of the value of the dollar. "The studio represents the kind of music that is adventuresome and is supported in Europe. . . . Whereas in the States it's not."

Guitarist Nick Didkovsky remembers Pauline not as an administrator, but as a teacher who put together an "incredible" week-long session during the time that both were there. She could really shake a student out of his or her complacent views toward performing. Drawing from her background in martial arts (shotokan karate), her philosophy of music as meditation, and her principles of unifying performers and audience, Pauline challenged students to see group interaction in a whole new light.

"She worked with us as a group for three days before we even picked up our instruments," Nick recalls. "Her whole goal was to create a group before we created a musical group. If the group wouldn't work on a more abstract level, there's no way it could work on the concrete level of playing."

She accomplished this by putting the group through a series of "very powerful exercises that had to do with meditation, and had to do with group interaction, and reaction exercises that [had] very simple, simple rules." As an example, Nick described the group, twenty-five strong, standing in a circle, holding hands, and propagating a pulse through the circle. Pauline would squeeze the hand of the person on her right. As soon as that person felt the squeeze, he or she would transfer it to the next person on the right, at the same time making some kind of vocal sound, until it went fully around. The intention was to see how quickly the pulse could be transferred throughout the group— how close to simultaneous they could make the total number of squeezes.

"Her whole thesis was that there are two ways to react to an impulse like that," says Nick. "You can pass it through your brain by recognizing it and then sending a signal to your other hand. Or you can pass a signal through another bundle of nerves, which is closer to your middle, your solar plexus. That's the really fast way to do it. . . .

"She talked about it, and we all got faster at passing it through. . . . I didn't know how well it was working for me, until once that afternoon, I felt like it passed through the channel that she was recommending. And it was like an electric shock—it was incredible!"

1982

The 1981-82 New Year's Intensive with Jack DeJohnette, Dave Holland, and Pat Metheny was the occasion of a rare event in CMS's history: a sold-out concert. New Year's Eve with this extraordinary trio drew an enthusiastic audience for what "was only the best jazz in town, the best jazz of its kind that you could ask to hear anywhere in the world." The audience member quoted here went on to say: "There's almost more pleasure in this music than I can bear. These guys are too good. It's so intimate! It almost hurts to hear it. You could cry."[1]

By April, though, the hurt that was felt around the Studio was far more tangible. Due to "a very serious cash flow problem" it became necessary to send the students home and close the session.

"It came down very fast," Karl told the *Woodstock Times.* "We didn't believe Reaganomics would be this bad. We were feeling the crunch. We felt we had to close the session early so we could concentrate on continuing in the future, selling the property, finding new spaces to move to." The task of selling Oehler's Mountain Lodge became as high a priority as buying it had been in 1976. Karl claimed that he was "running a first-class music program and a third-rate hotel. About 90 percent of our meeting time was about the hotel. I want out of the hotel business."[2]

---

1. Jim Reed, "A Good Beginning: New Year's Eve at the Creative Music Studio." *Woodstock Times*, January 7, 1982.

2. Peter Blum, "CMS Goes with the Cash Flow," *Woodstock Times*, April 22, 1982.

Although Oehler's had originally been acquired to accommodate what was becoming an "overwhelming" enrollment, the student population that April numbered only twelve. Karl attributed the overall decline to the fact that overseas students were unable to afford to come. Fewer American students were coming because of the pinch in the domestic economy, and foundations were finding it necessary to withhold grants or greatly decrease their amounts.

Nonetheless, Karl kept on pushing. At the same time that he found it necessary to close CMS's spring 1982 session, he was busily planning for the fourth Summer World Music Seminar, another Reggae Festival, and the second of what was originally hoped to be an annual series of Woodstock Jazz Festivals. Unfortunately, there never was another Woodstock Jazz Festival. On the other hand, the World Music Seminar, with the assistance of the National Endowment for the Arts, had become a certainty. It did happen—from June 14 through July 24.

On the 26th of June, Karl took the Music Universe Orchestra to perform at New York City's Kool Jazz Festival in a jazz and world-music concert, billed as "Music from Five Continents." The concert featured Paul Horn on solo flute; Rainbow, John Handy's group with L. Subramaniam, Ashish Khan, and Pranesh Khan; Codona, the Don Cherry-Nana Vasconcelos-Collin Walcott trio, this time augmented with saxophonist Jim Pepper; and the twenty-eight piece Music Universe Orchestra.

Jazz "stars," world-music heavyweights, and CMS "students" made this incarnation of the Music Universe Orchestra something extraordinary: Karl Berger, Ingrid Berger, Lee Konitz, Randy Brecker, Dave Liebman, Leroy Jenkins, Ed Blackwell, Gary Windo, Mark Helias, Paul McCandless, Collin Walcott, Steve Gorn, Nana Vasconcelos, Aiyb Dieng, Trilok Gurtu, Faruk Tekbilek, Peter Kowald, James Harvey, Ellen Ohm, Tom Cora, Ann Sheldon, Janet Grice, Sue Pilla, Peter Buettner, Jim Hartog, Tom Varner, and dancers Savia Berger and Atsuko Yuma.

Unfortunately, there is no recording of this concert in the CMS archives. But it was an excellent tie-in with the Studio's World Music Seminar. It brought added media recognition of CMS as a center for the burgeoning world-music movement.

There was a fall session in 1982, and CMS was still alive. It was clear, though, that the Studio was operating on a shoestring and that it was offering only a fraction of the workshops, concerts, and community events that Woodstockers and their neighbors had come to expect. For the first time since 1975-76, there was no New Year's Intensive. Activities became so sparse that when the 1983 Summer World Music Seminar got off the ground, it was referred to as a "CMS revival."[3]   It was, perhaps, the Studio's most significant event of the year, but it portended no real revival.

Welcome House

It was about this time in 1983 when Karl and Ingrid moved back to Mt. Tremper, to a place called the Welcome House, which was actually on the property of the old Lutheran Camp. That property had been divided into two parcels, one of 200 acres and one of 100 acres. A Zen Buddhist group acquired the larger parcel, which included the large stone building that had previously housed CMS. This soon became the Zen Arts Center and later, simply, the Zen Monastery. Karl and Ingrid acquired the smaller one, which included the Welcome House.

Karl recalls that "the idea at the time was to develop the spiritual aspect of CMS by working together with the Zen Arts Center. Zen art students, as far as they were related to music, would also do CMS sessions—it would all intertwine in some ways. So, that was really the basic idea that got us to go out to Welcome House."

There were some sessions that had Karl, trombonist Roswell Rudd, and others teaching music, while the students also studied Zen. Ultimately, the free-spirited CMS outlook and the strictness of Zen discipline had to go in different directions. "It was sort of an ideal idea in way," says Karl. "The very idea of Zen is very conducive to the basic practice that we did. But, the Japanese Zen tradition is very strict and requires certain postures and certain disciplines. . . . So there was some conflict arising—you know, people having to get up at 5:30, sitting straight and getting whacked. We were more drawn to the Tibetan style, which we had made contact with in the mid-seventies at Naropa. [The Tibetans] were much more relaxed in their way. They were just talking about mind training. . . . "

The other problem was that the organization in Los Angeles that oversaw the Zen group was pushing very hard for the Zen Arts Center to become primarily a monastery. The arts center was to become a smaller program of the overall monastic mission, and this is the way it is today. "So, philosophically and otherwise, we just drifted apart," says Karl.

As 1984 rolled around, the output of the Creative Music Studio had dwindled to a sporadic series of concerts and weekend workshops. Many of these concerts were billed as parties (the Taurus Party, the

---

3. Peter Blum, "CMS Revival," *Woodstock Times*, July 21, 1995, p. 43.

Aries Party, the Gamala Taki Party) and featured the Gamala Taki Band, a somewhat funked-up, electrified version of what the locals had come to know as Karl Berger and Friends. Karl and Ingrid were joined by Dave Brubeck's son Danny on drums, guitarist Dave Mason, and a variety of occasional percussionists, electric bassists, and horn players. A joint series of concerts put on by CMS and the Ulster County Council for the Arts presented Karl and Ingrid, Baikida Carroll, Pauline Oliveros, and others. And there were music-mind training sessions in April and May. Unfortunately, by the summer, CMS had closed the doors at Oehler's Mountain Lodge and ended all formal sessions with students in residence.

Rick Tarantelli, a drummer from upstate New York, has the distinction of being the last CMS participant to leave. Rick, like so many others, had come as a student and stayed on, contributing every type of assistance that he was capable of. He came in the spring of 1979 and soon found himself trading work for room and board. His first job was as a lifeguard at the pool. From there he moved into the office to do clerical, secretarial, and telephone work. He then took over the responsibility of computerizing and maintaining CMS's mailing list. He worked the door at concerts; he worked backstage at concerts; and he did a lot of the leg work to assemble a CMS archives/reading room/record collection. Rick, who was known as "Tranch" at the time, saw it all happen from 1979 until the very end.

In fact, the job of actually closing up CMS fell to Rick and Ingrid. Karl was in the Philippines, and when the time came to move boxes out and lock the doors, Rick and Ingrid were the only two around. "I couldn't have done it without him," Ingrid says. His style had always been to be "all over at the Studio, helping out, supporting people." After the close he remained a friend and supporter of Karl and Ingrid. Ingrid calls him "more than a friend. He's like a brother."

Karl carried on with a series of fall weekend intensives at Welcome House. By this time, the esteemed drummer and jazz veteran Jimmy Cobb had come to Woodstock. He, saxophonist Dave Liebman, trombonist Roswell Rudd, Olatunji, Congolese percussionist Tatitos Sompa, and dancer Carol Dowd made these weekends exciting, world-class events, despite the fact CMS had effectively closed up shop.

Back on the Road

Although the close of CMS in 1984 was a setback for the world creative-music community, it released Karl Berger from the burdens of being an administrator. There was, however, the burden of a massive debt, which was to accompany him for many years. He became free to travel, to focus on being a performer, and to take CMS-style teaching to the world rather than having the world come to Woodstock. "I went all over the place," says Karl. "It was, then, time to try the principles—all the world-music stuff that we had developed—to see what happens when we do that in other countries. That was really the direction that I took, then."

His travels actually began in 1983, when he, Ingrid, and Olatunji took a group to Africa. "In every African country," Olatunji recalls, "we went and performed with the people, the musicians. . . . We were well received. It was arranged so that we would perform with the native musicians. If there was any jazz group, we did programs together. That kind of thing, that kind of program needs to be supported, so the credit cannot just be given to people like Paul Simon, who did [things with] Ladysmith Black Mambazo. People like Karl and myself, we've been doing it, but we never get any support."

The CMS/Brazilian connection had developed to such a point that Karl was able to arrange to do three-week training sessions at Rio DeJaniero's Museum of Modern Art, three years in a row. This new South American phase of CMS on the road was aided by the presence of Ricardo Oliviera, a long-time CMS student. Ricardo had established CMS-style training in several different Brazilian locations. In doing so, he created the type of demand among local musicians that allowed Karl to come in and get a "great response."

Babatunde
Olatunji,
Oehler's Mt.
Lodge, 1983.

16

The Legacy

"All I can say is, it changed my life. It was meant to be; I was drawn here. Step after step led me to CMS, and it's been my community and my family ever since then. Karl and Ingrid and their daughters have been like family to me. It was a connection that was meant to be. The same people that I met, then, are still my closest friends, now. And that's been the really important thing—the community that's come out of this, [as well as] the urge to learn and develop, and the spiritual quest about the whole thing. Karl and Ingrid were always attuned to that; and the artists that they brought, and the artists that they loved and exposed people to always had that searcher's mentality, a searcher's soul. That was always an inspiration—that you realized that it wasn't [about] getting the next gig or attaining a certain level of musicianship, but that there was more going on, and music is a transmission of something. I'll never forget the poster that Ingrid had made. It said, 'Music is the healing force of the Universe.' And I think that was more of a central tenet to them than any kind of accomplishment—that you should practice music as a healing force and as an offering to people. And that, to me was the greatest teaching. The people who picked up on that were the luckiest ones."

—Peter Buettner

Peter Buettner, flutist and saxophonist with Woodstock's own Futu Futu (who performed at the big Woodstock II festival in 1994) is a part of the core network of CMS people who remain and produce vital work in or near Woodstock. Rick Tarantelli is also a member of Futu Futu and an active member of the local reggae scene. Jack DeJohnette, Dave Holland, Carla Bley, and Karl and Ingrid are still there, as are Steve Gorn, Marilyn Crispell, Tom Schmidt, Ilene Marder, and Marianne (Boggs) Collins and Tom Collins. Garry Kvistad continues to build Woodstock Percussion, Inc. and to perform benefit concerts for the Woodstock Guild. He recently bought a set of Balinese gamelan instruments and has formed a local gamelan orchestra. Through a nonprofit organization that he established, Garry has been able to hire a Balinese instructor for the group. Flutist Sue Pilla also lives in Woodstock and is part of that orchestra.

I was surprised to find out, when I was in Woodstock in August of 1994, just how many former CMS people had a hand in putting on Woodstock '94—surprised because of the seeming incongruity between the spirit of CMS and that of an enormous, commercial, rock-and-roll venture such as the festival. It became apparent, though, that no one was out of place or out of character. Marianne Boggs, administrator extraordinaire, was there as the cultural liaison for former Governor Mario Cuomo. Ilene Marder worked for Woodstock Ventures, coordinating and putting out public relations materials. Tom Schmidt and Ingrid were there, on stage, chanting and playing traditional instruments with the Tibetan Buddhist monks from the Karma Triyana Dharmachakra, which Tom administers. Tom had hoped to get Karl on stage to do basic gamala taki practice with the hundreds of thousands in attendance, but it didn't come to be.

However, this community that Peter refers to in the quote above merely originated at CMS; its reach is worldwide. Those who have been affiliated with CMS comprise a network of musicians—performers, teachers, composers, recording artists—that literally spans the globe. Other alumni have branched out into ancillary fields as recording engineers, concert promoters, instrument builders, writers, or film makers. Peter Apfelbaum concisely expresses the breadth of CMS's influence by saying, "Almost anyone I could mention has some tie to the Creative Music Studio."

CMS was like a world-music dispatcher: It drew musicians from all over the world, provided the right environment for them to form associations and to create together, and then returned them to where they had come from with an enlivened spirit to spread the message of music.

Still Going

Groups were formed at CMS that have endured on a professional level and are still out there contributing. I mentioned the String Trio of New York earlier. This is without question the longest-lasting collaboration to come out of CMS.

Curlew is another group that has endured, although they have not worked continuously. George Cartwright put Curlew together with CMS people right after he left CMS. The group is George's "idea of a dance music band." The many personnel changes over the years have brought George together with the likes of Bill Laswell, Tom Cora, Bill Bacon, David Moss, Philip Wilson, Denardo Coleman, Anton Fier, and Wayne Horvitz. The sixth Curlew album was recorded in January 1995.

"Find your own voice," is the advice that Karl gave to Larry Chernicoff and which has spurred Larry to maintain the Larry Chernicoff Quintet over the years. "Just play your own music," Karl told him, "and ten years from now, what you'll be doing is playing your own music. Only it'll be ten years stronger." Larry considers this the "single most important lesson that I learned." He decided, upon leaving CMS, that he would faithfully follow his own direction. And this is what he has done. "One of the main reasons for that was that I certainly can't play Thelonious Monk tunes any better than fifteen-hundred other people have done," Larry admits, "and probably a lot worse. I have some chance of being able to play music that I write."

The Larry Chernicoff Quintet has been playing Larry's tunes for over thirteen years, the last ten with the same personnel: Tom Schmidt on bass, Donnie Davis on saxophones (Larry and Donnie go way back together to the early days of CMS, when they were in the Woodstock Music and Dance Ensemble—Muanda), Tim Moran on woodwinds, and Tony Vacca, "a master of the African balaphon," on percussion.

Larry went on to expand his interpretation of the philosophical importance of the CMS experience: "It wasn't just about music. It was about creating a fertile ground for people to come and discover their path."

The commitment and dedication that the spirit of CMS instilled in people pushed them to develop skills required by the Studio, and themselves, for survival. Larry developed his skills in graphic design in this way. The need for posters and flyers to announce weekly CMS events gave him the opportunity to learn the craft and gave him enough training to later start his own graphic-design business. Other skills that Larry and others took away from CMS were in the area of self-design—skills in meditation, mind-body integration, spirituality, nutrition, and self-discipline. The environment made these all accessible, but no one was required to pursue them.

Dr. Nerve is sort of a "fractured fusion band, sort of John McLaughlin meets Stravinsky meets Zappa," according to Michael Lytle, clarinetist and one-time, live-in, full-time, do-everything sort of CMS guy. Michael has been with the band since its inception and has been on all of Dr. Nerve's recordings (in addition to developing his own solo career), but the actual creator of Dr. Nerve is guitarist Nick Didkovsky.

"CMS really started something with me and with so many people," Nick says. He came to the Studio much nearer the end than anyone else I spoke to. His first function was to record the Woodstock Jazz Festival in the fall of 1981. Dr. Nerve first performed in the fall of 1982. Since then the band, composed of two trumpets, bass clarinet, soprano saxophone, vibraphone, guitar, bass, and drums, has been to Europe nearly every year, and just released its sixth recording, "Skin."

Sadly, but typically, more Europeans have heard and seen this American band than have Americans. Creative American musicians have told me over and over again how much easier it is to get work in Europe and Japan, where support for the arts is considered a necessity and not a social liability.

Nick says, "It's easier for me to get eight people across the Atlantic to Europe and do a tour where everyone's making money and coming back having played to a lot of people, having been treated well—hotels, dinner, breakfast—the way it's supposed to be."

CMS in Hollywood

People who have come through CMS have carried the influence of music mind into nearly every realm of musical expression that can be conceived. Take Emily Hay, CMS's Hollywood connection, for example. Emily became involved with CMS when she was a student of classical flute and piano at Bard College, across the Hudson River from Woodstock. After a total immersion in the canon of classical flute music, Emily discovered jazz and had the opportunity to study with both Lee Konitz and Jimmy Giuffre at Bard. It was Jimmy Giuffre who convinced her to stick to the flute, rather than branch out to the saxophone. She expanded her improvisational skills with Don Cherry, Oliver Lake, Ed Blackwell, Dave Holland, and others as she went back and forth from Bard to CMS throughout her college years.

Emily then moved to California and pursued a master's degree at the California Institute for the Arts. However, her experiences at CMS inclined her naturally away from the classical music program and more toward the world music—Indian, African, Balinese—playing and studying situations.

She completed the master's program and pulled together all of her experiences to create a unique career in the Los Angeles music scene. She performs often in California with rock bands, as well as in Europe with musicians who would be considered avant garde, certainly well out of the mainstream. For a number of years Emily was an active concert promoter in L.A., bringing in Anthony Braxton, Roscoe Mitchell, Tom Cora, Leo Smith, and many lesser known performers.

In her "day gig," however, she wears a hat that makes her unique among all of the CMS people I've spoken to. "I supervise music for film and TV production," she told me. "I work with the producers and help them choose the music to go along with their productions, and then I do all the legal negotiations and set up all the contracts, soundtrack albums and stuff. . . . I recently did a film on Woodstock, and that was interesting because I had to track down a lot of artists from the sixties. . . . This was the second cut [of the well known commercial film on the festival], or the unreleased footage, produced by Jimi Hendrix' old producer, Alan Douglas." Watch for Emily's name in movie credits. She may be doing some Disney films in the near future.

Creative Advertising

Madison Avenue has also had the input of musicians who have been through CMS. Donnie Davis related to me his experiences creating jingles for a production company called Black Market, run by Woodstock musician and bandleader Marc Black. Marc was a CMS participant very early on, and he and his band performed often at CMS or at local events that featured CMS musicians.

"We'll do a Budweiser demo or something like that," says Donnie, "and then we'll do some other demo, and we'll have six hours of studio time booked up . . . in one of the best studios in New York. We'll call up a couple of friends and go down there, turn the lights out and just play. And the sound engineer becomes an equal member of the group; he manipulates the sound. . . . They edit things out, and if something sounds nice, they submit it for a demo for a Saab commercial or something. It's interesting stuff, not your typical jingle, that's for sure. These days [you might hear anything]. You could hear Ornette on a Nike commercial."

Studio Time

Students who have gone on from CMS to build recording studios have provided a valuable alternative to the commercial recording industry's "star-maker machinery." Pursuing a course of self-determination in music and disseminating the fruits of one's labors often begins with a supportive environment to record in. Tom Tedesco, of Paramus, New Jersey, came to CMS as a drummer. He found significant parallels between the CMS experience, which taught him how to "function as a human being," and the teaching traditions of India. "So much of what

Karl wanted to do here is a way of life in India," Tom feels. As a student and teacher of the tabla he now has a prime perspective from which to make that judgement.

With a good deal of help from Karl, Tom has set up a studio with an ambience that caters primarily to small jazz ensembles. "I have a nice piano, but it's not a huge place," says Tom. "I don't have a lot of electronic stuff here [and] the acoustic instruments seem to work really well in this setting."

Tom has recorded Dave Holland, Ed Blackwell, Joe Lovano, and a string of other artists whom he has contacted through his connection with Karl. "So many great artists—I couldn't even name them all. It's amazing that I've done so much work with people that I've really respected and looked up to," he adds.

Vinnie Martucci has a studio in Woodstock where Karl has done some of his most recent recordings. Vinnie, a pianist, was one of those few people who came to CMS with an extensive academic background and a thorough grounding in basic musicianship. Karl tapped into Vinnie's experience and asked him to teach harmony, theory, and ear training.

"From CMS I've entered into some real lifelong friendships and relationships," Vinnie told me. "I studied a lot with Baikida Carrol and Dave Holland. . . . I continued to study with Dave Holland for two years [after the close of CMS]. And at this point, now, I work with Baikida regularly. . . . He does a lot of writing for plays . . . and I act as an assistant for him. I'll play parts, record with him and act as an engineer and coproducer." It was Vinnie who introduced Karl to MIDI (musical instrument digital interface) and all of the possibilities in recording and editing using digital techniques. "This was in 1988 or '89," Vinnie recalls. "At that point [Karl] hadn't worked with it, cause it had only been around for a few years. So, he wasn't really quite familiar with how it worked. But once I explained it to him—how we could cut and paste all these different elements and just reuse them, turn them upside down, retrograde them, transpose them into different keys, whatnot, and just do it as sequence data—his eyes sort of lit up like Christmas trees!"

In 1987, Vinnie, drummer Dan Brubeck (Dave Brubeck's son), guitarist Mike DeMicco, and bassist Rob Leon formed a group called the Dolphins, which has recorded a number of CDs and tours regularly. Vinnie calls the group "one of my main focuses right now"—as if he didn't have enough main focuses already!

On the Air

You would think that creative music would be all over the National Public Radio airwaves. Although you'll hear more of it there than anywhere else, music of the innovators is in a constant struggle for airtime with music of decades ago—even on stations that emphasize a jazz presence.

There is at least one CMS alumnus currently on NPR playing the music of creative artists as much as his program manager and audiences will allow. (I tried to contact others but had no success.) Michael G. Nastos, of WEMU, an NPR affiliate at Eastern Michigan University, grew up in the same neck of the woods as I. We had never met until we both ended up at CMS. I had come out for the New Year's Intensive, 1978-1979, and Michael, a percussionist, had come out shortly before that to work in a CETA-funded position doing promotions and public relations and to take part in workshops.

Small world. Even smaller when you consider that Jim Quinlan, CMS program director from 1979 to 1981, started the jazz broadcasting program at WEMU, which, with Michael's input, has become one of the finest anywhere. Michael has also done considerable writing on jazz and contemporary music for Michigan and Midwest newspapers and periodicals. He has also wriitten for *Cadence, Down Beat, The All Music Guide*, and CD liner notes.

Academia

Although the classicists dominate the music-education programs at most universities (and this includes jazz education), creative musicians who have taught at CMS have made some inroads. Anthony Braxton holds a position at Wesleyan University, where he continues to teach his unique brand of composition and improvisation.

George Lewis is now at the University of California San Diego in a department labeled Critical Studies and Experimental Practices. His teaching is grounded in a philosophy that blends scholarship with his background in AACM-style self determination and creative freedom.

In his own words: "Something that I would like to see happen, now, in the university [would be] more of an open approach to music-making, including a kind of a scholarly dimension—generating scholarship, but also generating performances and generating communication, and the idea that improvised music, which was one of the primary focuses of CMS, could serve as a locus for exchange of cultures. . . . Karl did a very important thing, and it's certainly something that influences the way I teach, here."

Leo Smith is perpetuating a creative music presence at the California Institute for the Arts, by occupying a chair held previously by Anthony Braxton and Roscoe Mitchell. "I'm pretty fortunate, right now. I'm teaching in a school that trains people to be artists," says Leo. "The people that I have in my classes [are] generally about half the population of the jazz department and maybe 10 percent of the classical and world-music departments. What I'm trying to do with them is . . . to show them that in order to have an original thought, they have to understand the limits of information. And if all of them want to play tunes and stuff like that from the past, that's okay, but . . . I teach young artists that the only way to be remembered is to say something completely significant and that's beyond the frozen information that they've been given."

At the University of Michigan, jazz department head Ed Sarath teaches gamala taki practice, in addition to the music of Bird, Miles, Duke, and 'Trane. Drummer Andrew Cyrille teaches and pushes the "evolution of the music" at New York's New School for Social Research— where it all began in the late sixties with Karl's improvisation classes. Although Andrew Cyrille spent very little time teaching at CMS, his associations with Cecil Taylor and the whole New York "new music," "avant-garde" scene, as well as his associations with Karl, place him well in this group of creative-music educators. Garrett List and Frederic Rzewski are both teaching in Liege, Belgium, at the Conservatoire Royal de Musique. Bob Moses has private students at the New England Conservatory of Music in Boston, a school that has supplied CMS an ample corps of students and guiding artists. Basoonist Janet Grice, a member of the 1979 Woodstock Workshop Orchestra, is an active educator, working primarily with children in schools. She does workshops and classes through the Lincoln Center and Carnegie Hall, and her teaching is supported by symphony orchestras in and near New York City. At CMS, she distinguished herself by teaching kundalini yoga to the few stout-hearted souls who could get up early enough to take advantage of her classes.

Jim Quinlan, although not technically an educator, brings a wealth of creative music to Dade County Community College in Miami Florida, where he is the performing arts coordinator. He also heads up the Rhythm Foundation, a nonprofit organization that presents music from the Caribbean, South America, and Africa.

Karl is now a professor at the Hochschule für Musik und Darstellende Kunst in Frankfurt, Germany. Those who study with him there are fortunate enough to receive the same type of guidance in rhythm and tuning, composition and improvisation, large-ensemble and solo playing that made CMS unique.

In many ways, Karl's still doing what he was doing at CMS. He travels back and forth from Germany to Woodstock a number of times each year and conducts workshops all over the United States, South America, and Europe.

Allen Ginsberg, who teaches at Brooklyn College, brings up the point that in these times of budget cuts on all fronts, "Many schools are abandoning their wisdom teachings for commercial reasons. . . . So maybe there will be the need for some of these private schools [like CMS] to do wisdom teaching, ancient teaching or more personalized teaching than the mass-production [educational] factories."

Looking Back, Looking Ahead

To list all of the CMS musicians who are still active and to describe their activities would take us on for hundreds more pages. What is more important is to envision this interwoven, worldwide tapestry of musical creativity, which has connections, at every point, to the Creative Music Studio.

It reminds me of the movie and play "Six Degrees of Separation," which expounds the premise that no one person on the planet is removed from any other person by more than six people. This can easily be said of musicians and CMS: No musician on the planet is further removed than six musicians (at the most—probably fewer) from some musician who has a connection to the Creative Music Studio.

Despite the pervasiveness of this network of active, innovative, living, breathing, creative musicians, we have come to a point where the function of music in our lives is being fulfilled far too extensively through technology and the media. We hear primarily those sounds that have withstood the scrutiny of the marketplace as dictated by the recording industry. Our children are in danger of missing the fact that music is born of the souls of real people reaching out to others to lift up the human spirit. It is not created by boxes of speakers, electronic appliances, or little plastic disks.

Most of the cultures of the world whose music is now having such an impact on what we hear, those cultures whose musical influence is coming to be known as *world music*, have given music an essential, integral role in the rituals, ceremonies, and even the work of day-to-day life. It has not existed as entertainment. It has not been a product to buy and sell.

There is an endless variety of improvised music that is not being aggressively marketed by the recording industry, therefore not played on radio stations, and not chanced by concert promoters—all of which means that people are not hearing it. The businesspeople are not willing to risk the meager or nonexistet payoff.

The greater risk is that we lose touch with the fact that music has enriched the lives of humankind throughout history, and has been a marketable, wealth-building commodity for only a handful of decades. The greatest risk is that creative music be undervalued by our society.

"If anybody says there is no audience for it [creative music], they are a liar. It's just that nobody has the imagination to market it."

—Marilyn Crispell

When the recording industry was still young, in the fifties and sixties, it took chances. It put out experimental music. It recognized, accepted, and promoted (although certainly not in the way that performers are promoted today) the improvisers who were taking the music forward.

The conservatism of the eighties and nineties has dictated, however, that record companies stick with the tried and true. They market primarily that which can be conveniently packaged. And in improvised music that package has come to be what is generally regarded as "classic" jazz by an audience that has been deprived of the richness of options in a music that has always been characterized by searching and experiment. Music that is evolutionary, by definition, cannot be called classic. Could Eric Dolphy get a record deal today?

CMS was the embodiment of a spirit of community and creativity that has gone dormant. I say dormant because musical tastes and conservative trends have shown themselves to be cyclical. They come and go and come around again. Human creativity will not be suppressed.

For now, we have become estranged from this spirit of music making that unabashedly holds itself up as a force for bringing people together—a force for change, a force for healing, a force for peace.

We are left wanting for a spirit that enables the formation of communities where music can be taught and experienced in the absence of competition and rancor. In the sixties and early seventies this spirit, this freedom of expression, was nurtured and encouraged by artists and audiences. It spawned music of unprecedented creativity.

Granted, some of the so-called free music experiments may be forgotten over time. Whether or not people are still listening to some of the "out" players seventy-five years from now is not of as great a consequence as the fact that an environment existed where they could explore.

Carl Sagan has said, "Often the technology that makes our civilization comes from basic 'impractical' research. Support for basic scientific research is vital for the future of humanity." I see a clear analogy between basic scientific research and the work done at CMS. The creative musicians whom I've been discussing are the basic researchers in music, and their work has pointed the way for our musical "civilization" to move forward. CMS was a laboratory where they were able to investigate.

Let the CMS legacy stand for courage as well—the courage to design one's own fate in spite of all opposition. Those who attended CMS (and, I hope, those who read this book) couldn't help but be affected in some way by the courage shown by Karl Berger and his family in making CMS a reality.

It was an all-consuming effort that had an impact on every aspect of their lives. Karl and Ingrid believed strongly in what CMS was all about. Again and again, people interviewed for this book echoed the contention that the Bergers' courage in making the sacrifices that they did, and taking the heat when things went wrong, was a real inspiration.

The message was loud and clear for all who were listening: Value your abilities, value your spirit, value your creativity. Have the courage to take risks, to try the hard thing. Have the courage to change, to distance yourself from situations that are not taking you toward your goals.

During one of the New Year's Intensive sessions with the Art Ensemble of Chicago, Joseph Jarman was listening to some students who had attended Berklee College of Music. He was hearing a good deal of disparagement for the experience at what they were calling "Berserklee."

"If they call the school Berserklee," Joseph wondered, "what must they think of themselves?" It was painful for many of the students to make the honest assessments of themselves that creating and growing in an intimate setting requires. However, associating with artists who had to believe in themselves in order to accomplish what they set out to do gave CMS students a strengthened confidence in their own abilities to create, whether it be in music, carpentry, poetry, or banking.

"Jazz has gone through quite some revolutions since Ornette Coleman, Cecil Taylor, Don Cherry, and Coltrane came on the scene. But future generations will know: None of them will be more lasting than the opening of jazz to the great musical cultures of the world."

—Joachim Berendt, coproducer of the "Jazz and World Music" portion of the 1982 Kool Jazz Festival

The world-music phenomenon is an inevitable evolutionary force. It would have occurred even if CMS hadn't. It can certainly be argued, though, that it began and blossomed there. CMS was the base camp for so many of the initial forays by the music's innovators into the realm of possibilities that the world-music force has revealed.

The Studio was meeting a need that no other study center for music has been able to or even tried to meet. There are and have been numerous study centers that can groom a musician for a successful career in recording commercial music. Music schools that train the finest technicians for reproducing the classic works have been around for hundreds of years.

Nowhere else, though, have musicians been availed of an environment where they were encouraged by some of the finest musicians in the world to, as saxophonist George Cartwright says, "try anything you want; let's find out the limits of who you are via the music—find out the limits of the music, if there are any."

Afterword

"We Need CMS Now More Than Ever"

I would like to congratulate Bob Sweet for putting together such a wonderful book of reminiscence. It brings many points to the forefront that are still urgent and burning issues today.

When CMS had to close its doors, I thought: There are many people now who will carry these ideas into other institutions, and maybe CMS as a center will not be needed any longer. But as Roscoe Mitchell aptly states: "We need it now more than ever." Music education has turned more conservative in recent years. The institutions may provide excellent stylistic training, but they mostly fail to foster and encourage personal creativity where it wants to unfold and flourish.

I feel that the time has come to embark on Phase II of the CMS journey. CMS now has a great legend to build upon. The people who encountered the CMS experience want to see it continue and be available to coming generations. The decisive difference is that we can now carefully plan a long-term development.

My vision is to begin with a bare piece of land, large and secluded enough to accommodate all the structural and functional needs of a CMS campus, that we can slowly grow into. And with enough space to build a community of artists and friends who would like to have a permanent place there and add their names to the future of CMS. There is an actual site near Woodstock being offered, where friends of CMS may purchase private building land and thereby help to make this vision a solid reality. There is no hurry. This time it can be done in a way that will survive the political-economic changes and will remain on a sure footing.

The new CMS will not only be a center of learning,

experimentation, and research, but also one of production, recording and communication, with equal emphasis on personal creativity. Recorded works of enduring quality, as well as the "Emerging Artists" series that we always had in our plans, will become a reality, guided by a policy of long-term values and perseverance.

I would like to invite your active or supportive membership and participation in the Creative Music Foundation. Together we can literally build a solid foundation for the CMS experience for generations to come.

As the world appears to turn faster, speedier, and ever more competitive, we need to feel and provide a sense of unhurried space, where creativity is allowed to unfold and manifest in limitless dimensions, guided by personal discipline and genuine spontaneity.

Karl Berger
Creative Music Foundation
Woodstock, NY 12498-0671

Bibliography

This is a listing of select references to publications relevant to CMS. The bulk of these are articles from newspapers in Woodstock, Kingston, greater Ulster County, and Albany, New York. There are, however, items from national and international publications that provide excellent views of CMS and do not require traveling to Ulster County to locate. Citations that are incomplete were taken from clippings in the CMS archives that do not include full information.

"AEC at CMS." *The Good Times*, December 12-15, 1978.
[Art Ensemble of Chicago].
"All That Jazz!" *The Daily Freeman*, September 21, 1981.
[Woodstock Jazz Festival photo with long caption].
Allen, Neal. "Art Group Claims Bias in Secret CETA Memos." *The Daily Freeman,* September 4, 1980.
_____. "Karl Berger and the Process of World Music." *The Daily Freeman,* August 24, 1981.
_____. "Last Word on CETA and Arts is Delayed." *The Daily Freeman,* September 5, 1980.
Andersen, Eric. "The First Woodstock Jazz Festival: And a Conversation with Karl Berger." *Woodstock Times*, September 3, 1981, p.44.
_____. "Let the Reggae Into Your Life." *Woodstock Times,* August 27, 1981,
"Audiences Should Be Given More Musical Information to Enhance Appreciation." *The Calgary Herald,* December 12, 1980.
[CMS at Banff].
"Avant Garde, Jazz Debuts at CMS." *The Daily Freeman,* November 13, 1980, p. 10.
[Tamia, Marion Brown, LaDonna Smith, Davey Williams at CMS].

"Beat Goes on at Kleinert." *The Daily Freeman,* June 28, 1980.
    [Aiyb Dieng, Collin Walcott].

Berger, Karl. "Letter To the Editors." *Woodstock Times,* October 1,
    1981.

Bers, Anne. "At the Creative Music Foundation, Quiet is the Key."
    Kite, June 4, 1980, p. 5.

Blum, Peter. "CMS Goes with the Cas Flow." *Woodstock Times,*
    April 22, 1982.

_____. "CMS Revival." *Woodstock Times,* July 21, 1983, p. 43.

_____. "The David Oliver Project." *Woodstock Times,* November 19,
    1987, p. 26.
    [Review of concert at Kleinert with Karl Berger, Dave Mason,
    and Dan Brubeck]

_____. "Gasser and Gamala." *Woodstock Times,* April 19,
    1984, p. 50.
    [Aries Party at Welcome House].

_____. "Jazz from the Heart." *Woodstock Times,* June 4,
    1987, p. 40.
    [Review of concert at Kleinert with Karl Berger, Ed
    Blackwell, and Frank Luther].

_____. "Lee Konitz's Good Pick-Up Band." *Woodstock Times,*
    July 11, 1985, p. 59
    [Lee Konitz, Dan Brubeck, Karl Berger, Frank Luther]

_____. "Opposite Ends of Town." *Woodstock Times,* July 15,
    1982, p. 40.
    [Review of Olatunji at CMS].

_____. "Playing it by Ear: Creative Music Studio Improvises Its
    Destiny." *Woodstock Times,* April 13, 1989, p. 1.

_____. "Springtime in the Arts." *Woodstock Times,* March
    22, 1984, p. 36.
    [Announcements of performances by Karl Berger, Marilyn
    Crispell, Ingrid Sertso, Gamala Taki Band].

_____. "Steve Gorn and Peter Wharton." *Woodstock Times,*
    December 5, 1985, p. 31.
    [Concert review].

Blumenthal, Bob. "New Music Goes to Church." *The Boston Phoenix,*
    January 25, 1977, p. 6.

Brennam, Brian. "Music Makers Meet: Musicians Gather in Banff to
    Probe Many Mysteries of Improvisation." *The Calgary Herald,*
    December 12, 1980, p. 14.

Bresnan, Debra. "Hypnorhythms: Master Jazz Vibist and Hip
    Hypnotherapist Cook Up a Music Workshop." *Woodstock Times,*

September 10, 1992, p. 1.

[Karl Berger and Peter Blum].

"Cecil Taylor Unit: A New Year's Celebration." *The Daily Freeman,*
December 30, 1979.

"Change in C.M.S. Format." *Woodstock Times,* January 15, 1976.

"CMS Celebrates New Year." *The Daily Freeman,* December 28, 1981.

[Photo of Dave Holland with caption about concert].

"CMS Explains Awards." *The Daily Freeman,* April 10, 1981, p. 9.

[Announcement of grant-application process given by
Creative Arts Public Service Program].

"CMS Lists Concerts." *The Daily Freeman,* October 24, 1980,

[Jay Clayton, Evan Parker, Derek Bailey].

"C.M.S. Presents Everything: Stu Martin Discusses Where
It's All Coming From." *Woodstock Times,* February 13, 1975,

Cohen, Joe. "Passing Over: Cecil Taylor and Memories of my
Underdevelopment." *Hartford Advocate,* April 10, 1985, p. 25.

Coleman, Mark. "Residency Brief but Buoyant." *The Michigan Daily,*
December 2, 1979, p. 7.

[Karl Berger in residence at University of Michigan].

"Community Picnic at CMS." *Woodstock Times,* August 17, 1978.

"Concert Series with a Difference." *The Daily Freeman,* October 9, 1978.

[Mentions poetry with Allen Ginsberg, Ann Waldman, Ed
Sanders, and Janine Pommy Vega].

"County Wide Festival Open to Local Group." *The Daily Freeman,*
June 8, 1980,

"Creative Music: Electronics." *Kite,* July 12, 1978,

[Announcement of Rzewski, Teitelbaum concert July 15].

"Creative Music Foundation." *Down Beat* (Spring 1975).

[*Down Beat* Daily, Spring '75].

"Creative Music Foundation." *Woodstock Times,* June 23, 1977.

"Creative Music Foundation." *Swing Journal* 30, no. 6
(June 1976): 76.

"Creative Music Studio Tuning Up for Dollars: $187,000 Fund Drive
Eyed to Purchase Oehler's Lodge." *The Daily Freeman,*
December 1, 1976, p. 2.

Culp, Marguerite. "Has the Magic Gone?" *Woodstock Times,*
August 27, 1981, p. 1.

[Woodstock scene, CMS, Overlook Press, etc.].

"Dave Holland Sidelined." *Woodstock Times,* September 10, 1981.

DiNardo, Robert. "Karl Berger." *Coda* 11, no. 12 (October 1974): 2-6.

[Interview].

"A Dream Changes: It's a Long Way from Mead's Mountain House to Oehler's Mountain Lodge." *Woodstock Times,* November 4, 1976, p. 1.

"Drummer to Thump at CMS." *The Daily Freeman,* November 20, 1980, p. 16.
[Ed Blackwell].

Evans, Ellayn M. "Keyboard News: Cecil Taylor Residency." *Contemporary Keyboard* (December 1979): 97.

Evers, Alf. *Woodstock: History of an American Town* (Woodstock: Overlook, 1987).

Faber, Harold. *The New York Times,* August 31, 1979.
[Sun Energy Festival].

Feldman, Mitchell. "CMS: A Forum for Experimentation." *Woodstock Times,* September 22, 1979.

_____. "Gary Windo: Sound that Would Scare the Alien." *Woodstock Times,* July 26, 1979.

_____. "Joseph Jarman: The Complete Performer." *Woodstock Times*, August 2, 1979, p. 31.

_____. "Nana Vasconcelos at CMS." *Woodstock Times,* July 19, 1979.

_____. "Sun Energy Festival at CMS." *Woodstock Times,* August 30, 1979.

"Films and Film-Makers at Creative Music Studio." *Woodstock Times*, March 5, 1981.

"Flute Farmers: Program on Village Green Last Saturday." *Woodstock Times,* June 11, 1981, p. 24.
[Harvey Sollberger].

Gerber, Leslie. "CMS Goes Baroque." *Woodstock Times,* December 15, 1977.

_____. "Frederic Rzewski & The Philharmonic." *Woodstock Times,* November 18, 1976.
[Concert review].

_____. "Genius and Torture at CMS." *Woodstock Times,* January 10, 1980.

_____. "G.S. Sachdev at the Kleinert Gallery." *Woodstock Times,* December 27, 1979.

Gilbert, Craig. "Hurley Quiets Concert Fears." *The Daily Freeman,* August 26, 1980, p. 4.
[Bonnie Raitt concert].

Gottlieb, Sidney. "Rzewsky [sic] Broke New Ground." *The Daily Freeman*, April 17, 1979, p. 8.

"Grachan Moncur III at CMS." *Riffs,* July 27-August 9, 1978, p. 3.

Hajosy, Dolores. "Creative Music Studio: Home of Universal Sound."

Visions 1, no. 1 (Spring 1982): 36.
["A quarterly publication of works by contemporary minority artists, photographers, writers and craftspeople. . . . Made possible by a grant from New York State CETA. . . . published by Kingston Artists Group, Kingston, New York"].

Hayes, Stephen. "Show-and-Tell: The Ulster County Council for the Arts Tests Its New Direction." *Woodstock Times,* July 24, 1980, p. 8.

Henderson, Edwina. "CETA and Arts Spawn Country Fest." *The Daily Freeman,* July 25, 1980, p. 9.

————. "Ex-prof Makes Noise His Living." *The Daily Freeman,* December 30, 1979.
[Garry Kvistad].

Hopkins, Michael F. "In the Poetry and Tradition of the Music." *The Spectrum,* October 28, 1977, p. 15.

"HVP at CMS." *Riffs,* August 10-23,
[Huron Valley Philharmonic].

"Improvisation and Composition Studies: Described as a Combination of Many Forms." *Woodstock Times,* May, 1973.

Isenberg, Sheila. "Woodstock Library Fair Fulfills Great Expectations—Nets $19G." *The Daily Freeman*, July 27, 1981.
[Ahmadu Jarr performs].

Jay, Chris. "The Way of Watazumido." *Woodstock Times,* October 8, 1981, p. 24.

"Jazz." *The Varsity,* March 1979.
[Review of Toronto concert with Karl Berger, Ingrid Sertso, and Mark Helins on bass].

"Jazz Benefit at Hurley." *The New York Times,* September 18, 1981.

"Jazz Festival: Sun Shines Through." *Woodstock Times,* October 1, 1981,

"Jazz Players Give Concert." *The Daily Freeman,* October 11, 1979, p. 19.
[Lee Konitz et al.].

"Jazzmen Gather for CMS Concerts." *The Daily Freeman*, November 7, 1980, p. 13.
[Steve Lacy, Peter Brotzmann, Louis Moholo, Harry Miller].

Johnson, Eve. "Berger Jazz Has Humor and Skill." *The Vancouver Sun,* September 1979.

Johnson, Tom. "Of Electronic Caricatures." *The Village Voice,* June 20, 1974, p. 52.
[Performances at Artists House].

Kalipolites, Marcus. "Esoteric Music in West Hurley Concert."

The Times Herald Record, June 26, 1979.

_____. "Percussionist Explores Sounds Not Usually Heard in Concert." *The Times Herald Record,* June 27, 1978, p. 46. [Jerome Cooper].

Kelly, Bob. "Arts Festival August 1; Hundreds of Artists Are Scheduled to Participate." *Woodstock Times,* July 24, 1980, p. 9.

Kelly, R. J. "Arts Coalition Demolition." *Woodstock Times,* September 11, 1980. [CETA].

_____. "Flute Master Captures Crowd." *The Sunday Freeman,* October 11, 1981, p. 1. [The Daily Freeman, Sunday edition; Watazumido Dozo Roshi].

"The Kool Jazz Festival: Jazz & World Music." *The Wisdom's Child New York Guide* (June 21-June 27, 1982).

Laing, Sara. "Colorful Background Combines in Vocalist's Voice." *The Daily Freeman,* December 11, 1985, p. 30. [Ingrid Sertso].

Lancashire, David. "Creative Rhythm in the Rockies." *The Globe and Mail,* Decmber 11, 1980, p. 7. [CMS at Banff].

Lee, David. "Creative Music Studio: Creative Music Studio, Woodstock, N.Y., December 31, 1979." *Coda* , no. 171 (1980). [Review of Cecil Taylor concert with students].

Leigh, Stuart. "African Music at the CMS." *Woodstock Times,* July 9, 1981, p. 33.

_____. "Interview: Karl Berger & Aiyb Dieng." *Ear Magazine* (July 1981).

"Leo Smith at CMS." *Woodstock Times,* May 1, 1980, p. 29.

"Library Fair this Saturday." *Ulster County Townsman,* July 23, 1981, p. 1. [*Woodstock Townsman,* alternate title].

Licht, Larry. "Karl Berger, York University, March 18, 1974." *Coda* (April, 1974).

Montgomery, Kitty. "A Discussion Via Percussion." *The Daily Freeman,* July 1, 1980, p. 7. [Aiyb Dieng, Collin Walcott].

_____. "Flute Farm Cultivates Fans on Village Green." *The Daily Freeman,* June 8, 1981, p. 11. [Harvey Sollberger].

Mullin, Patricia W. "Creative Music Studio: Beyond the Traditional." *River Valley Chronicle,* June 1979, p. 36.

"Music Festival." *The Village Voice,* May 30, 1974, [Performances at Artists House].

"Music, Music: Creative Music Studio Has a Full Concert Schedule."
    Woodstock Times, December 19, 1974,

"The New Music Settles in Woodstock: Creative Music Foundation Adds
    Yet Another Element to the Town's Musical Talent."
    Woodstock Times, October 11, 1973, p. 24.

Occhiogrosso, Peter. "Karl Berger: Music Universe c/o Woodstock, N.Y."
    Down Beat (June 3, 1976): 18.

———. "Vibes of a Different Hue." *The Village Voice,*
    May or July 23, 1974, p. 80.
    [Karl Berger profile].

"On Jazz: Berger's Bash." *Cash Box* 43, no. 20
    (October 3, 1981).

"The Peace Church Concerts: Karl Berger, Ing Rid, Dave Holland and
    Friends (Creative Music Communication — CMC 1)." *Insider,*
    September 1975, p. 45.
    [Record review].

Pilla, Sue. "The Educated Ear." *Woodstock Times,* December 24,
    1980, p. 10.
    [Interview with Dave Holland].

Plakias, Mark. "Where Teaching Meets Jamming." *Jazz Magazine* 3,
    no. 1 (Fall 1978): 28.

"Random Notes." *Rolling Stone* (August 9, 1979).
    [Ed Sanders' "Karen Sikwood Cantata" at CMS].

Rapp, Rodger. "Gimme Shelter: Three Days of Art, Dreams, And Rain,
    Rain, Rain. . ." *Woodstock Times,* August 7, 1980, p. 23.
    [County-wide arts festival].

———. "Photographic Rhythms at Creative Music Studio."
    Woodstock Times, April 24, 1980, p. 11.

Reed, Jim. "A Good Beginning: New Year's Eve at the Creative
    Music Studio." *Woodstock Times*, January 1982.

———. "Music as a Way of Life: The New Music at the Creative
    Music Studio." *Woodstock Times*, August 3, 1978, p. 17.

———. "Notes from Underground: Colloquium at Creative Music
    Studio on "How Does a Musician Make a Living?""
    Woodstock Times, August 3, 1978, p. 19.

———. "Talk About the Way." *Woodstock Times*, October 8, 1981,
    p. 25.
    [Interview with Pauline Oliveros, Karl Berger, and others
    talking about Watazumi Dozo Roshi].

———. "Total Theater in Solo Sax and Flute at CMS."
    Woodstock Times, August 9, 1979, p. 26.
    [Review of Joseph Jarman concert with Peter Apflebaum].

_____. "Up and Down the Town and Out." *Woodstock Times,*
 August 13, 1981,
 [Events around town; Vinnie Martucci and friends at the
 Threepenny].

"Reggae Festival at CMS." *The Daily Freeman,* August 1981.

Remsnyder, Rick. "Carlos Santana: Everything is Now Clear."
 The Daily Freeman, August 31, 1978, p. 27.

Rockwell, John. "Music: Jazz Fuses with Avant-Garde." *The New York
 Times,* January 1978.
 [Review of Leo Smith, CMS Orchestra, and others at
 Carnegie Hall].

"Roscoe Mitchell at CMS." *Riffs,* July 13-26, 1978, p. 5.

Rothbart, Peter. "Orchestrating the Collective Consciousness: Cecil
 Taylor at the Creative Music Studio." *Down Beat*
 (April 1980): 17.

Schachter, Ellen. "Common Energy Evolves in Music Studio."
 The Daily Freeman, July 5, 1979, p. 11.

Schonberg, Harold C. "Nuggets from 1978 You May Have Missed."
 The New York Times, January 7, 1979.
 [CMS concert in Kentucky's Mammoth Caves].

"School of Classical Indian Music Looking to Set Up Local Classes."
 Woodstock Times, October 4, 1973.
 [Vasant Rai].

Smith, Arnold Jay. "Creative Music Studio Benefits From 1st
 Woodstock Jazz Fest." *Billboard Magazine* (October 10, 1981).

_____. "Reaching for the Cosmos: A Composers'
 Colloquium." *Down Beat* (October 20, 1979): 19.

_____. "Traditions Upheld and Broken at Jazz School Near
 Woodstock." *Billboard Magazine* (April 10, 1982).

Solothurnmann, Jurg. "Karl & Ingrid Berger: "Music Universe" in
 Woodstock." *Jazz Forum* (1979).

Sprick, Tomm. "Creativity—Aim of New Foundation." *Herald
 News,* July 25, 1972.

Stackel, Leslie. "Trips fpr the Real Trouper." *Apartment Life*
 (July 1978): 14.

Stern, Andrea Barrist. "Bonnie Raitt Attracts 2600 at CMS."
 Woodstock Times, August 28, 1980, p. 42.

"Steve Lacy Quintet." *Woodstock Times,* September 6, 1980, p. 31.

Terry, Kenneth. "Jazz and Classical Musicians Interact at Woodstock."
 The New York Times, July 23, 1978.

"Through a Plastic Glass Darkly." *Woodstock Times,* April 10, 1980.
 [Art exhibit at CMS].

"Trio of Performances at Creative Music Studio." *The Daily Freeman,* May 16, 1979, p. 14.

Trump, Peter. "Second Woodstock: Bach to Joplin." *Times-Union,* August 13, 1978, p. 8.

"Two Faces of Jazz." *Woodstock Times,* January 2, 1975, p. 10-11.

Urban, Georgia. "Auld Lang Syne Many Ways." *The Entertainer,* December 26, 1980, p. 24. [Sam Rivers, Dave Holland New Year's Intensive].

_____. "Braxton Makes Music with Mathematics." *The Entertainer,* August 24, 1979, p. 9.

_____. "Catskill Jazz Fest Ends Summer." *Knickerbocker News,* September 1, 1981, p. 11.

_____. "Creative Music Studio Offering Spring Workshops in Woodstock." *Knickerbocker News,* March 14, 1979, p. 7.

_____. "Creative Music Studio Showcase for World Music." *Knickerbocker News,* July 17, 1981, p. 5.

_____. "Georgia on Jazz." *Knickerbocker News,* July 12, 1978, p. 7.

_____. "Georgia on Jazz." *Knickerbocker News,* August 23, 1978.

_____. "Georgia on Jazz." *Knickerbocker News,* August 9, 1978, p. 7.

_____. "Georgia on Jazz." *Knickerbocker News,* August 3, 1978, p. 8.

_____. "Georgia on Jazz." *Knickerbocker News,* March 5, 1980. [Spring session announcement].

_____. "Georgia on Jazz." *Knickerbocker News,* April 1, 1981. [CETA].

_____. "Making Music in a Monastery." *Troy Herald Record,* June, 1976.

_____. "Things to Come." *The Entertainer*, December 21, 1979. [Cecil Taylor].

_____. "Verstaile DeJohnette Changes Directions." *The Entertainer,* November 23, 1979, p. 4.

_____. "Woodstock Studio "Intensive" to Feature Chicago Ensemble." *Knickerbocker News,* December 20, 1978, p. 6.

Van Chieri, Carole. "Karl Berger and the Creative Music Studio." *Woodstock Times,* April 18, 1974, p. 22.

Varty, Alex. "Karl Berger: Jazz Musician, Composer and Teacher." *Vancouver Free Press,* June 29-July 5, 1979, p. 15-16. [Interview].

_____. "Karl Berger: The Educator." *Vancouver Free Press,* October 1978.

(Watazumi Dozo Roshi at CMS). *Take-no-Michi* (Newsletter of Shakuhachi and Related Arts) (Summer 1981).

Wild, David. "Berger/Holland: 'All Kinds of Time,' Sackville

3010." *Coda* (June 1, 1978).

[Record review].

Winnegrad, Kay. "Sara Cook with CMS Group at WAA." *Woodstock Times,* May 16, 1974.

Wiser, John D. "Stood Up Again." *Woodstock Times,* July 5, 1984, p. 50.

[Review of NYU Contemporary Players at Welcome House].

"Woodstock Jazz Festival." *Woodstock Times,* August 13, 1981.

[Announcement].

"Woodstock to Get Jazz, Indian Music." *The Sunday Freeman,* March 27, 1983, p. 32.

[Ustad Jamaluddin Bhartiya].

"World Music Closes at CMS." *The Daily Freeman,* July 18, 1980, p. 6.

Zabor, Rafi. "Creative Music Studio." *Musician,* no. 40 (February 1982)

"Zorn and Chadbourne." *Woodstock Times,* April 24, 1980.

Index

Roach, Max, 7, 97
Rockefeller Foundation, 142
Romano, Aldo, 24
Rome, Italy, 50
Romeo, Max, 130
Roshi, Watazumido Dozo, 132-133
Rova Saxophone Quartet, 78
Roy, Badal, 130
Rudd, Roswell, 145, 146
Rudolph, Adam, 93, 127-129
Rundgren, Todd, 44
Russell, Arthur, 85-86
Russell, George, 50, 68, 73
Rzewski, Frederic, 50, 51, 62, 67, 68, 75, 95, 100-101, 111, 156

Sachdev, G.S., 123, 130
Sagan, Carl, 159
samba, 130
San Diego, California, 52, 142
San Francisco, California, 78, 108
Sanders, Ed, 52, 85, 94
Sanders, Pharaoh, 70
Santana, (Devadip) Carlos, 88
Santos, Jumma, 36, 68
Sarath, Ed, 36, 156
Schmidt, Tom, 50, 51, 55, 149, 150, 151
Schoenberg String Quartet, 75
Schoenberg, Arnold, 75
Schuller, Gunther, 26, 88
Schutz, George, 131
Scofield, John, 51
Sebastian, John, 44
Senegal, 122, 131
Sertso, Ingrid, 24, 26, 29-31, 36-37, 44, 51-53, 62, 68, 69, 70, 71, 86, 104, 118, 131, 144, 145, 146, 147, 149, 150, 159
shakuhachi flute, 17, 60, 132-133
Shankar, Lakshmi, 123
Shankar, Ravi, 7, 123
Sheldon, Ann, 144
Sierra Leone, 126
Silvan, Alan, 107
Simon, Paul, 147

Sines, Terry, 105
Siral, Ismet, 124, 126-127, 129, 130
"Six Degrees of Separation", 157
Smith, Leo, 38, 56, 61, 68, 70, 74, 86, 103, 153, 156; rhythm units, 72
Sompa, Tatitos, 146
"Songs of Innocence, Songs of Experience", 86
Sons of Creation, 131
Sousa, John Philip, 17
Space for Creative Development, 100
Space Orchestra, 100
Speculum Musicae, 74
Spirit Place, A, 44
spirituality, 24, 44, 45, 52, 151
srudi box. *See swar-peti*
Stravinsky, Igor 87, 151
String Trio of New York, 58, 150
Studio Time, 153
Subramaniam, L. 123, 144
Sufi music, 129-130
suijo, 132
Sun Ra, 70
Suso, Foday Musa, 126, 128, 130
Suspenders, The, 89
swar-peti, 37, 130
Swing Journal, 61

tabla, 84, 86, 97, 123, 130, 153
Talking Heads, 129
tamboura, 130
Tarantelli, Rick, 146, 149
Taurus Party, 145
Taylor, Cecil, 70, 72, 73-74, 107-110, 113, 116-117, 156, 160; Unit, 107-110
technology, 17, 159
Tedesco, Tom, 153-154
Teitelbaum, Richard, 9, 50, 51, 55, 100-101, 103, 104, 141
Tekbilek, Faruk, 126-127, 129, 130, 144
Tekbilek, Haci, 126-127, 129, 130
Thomas, Leon, 125
Threadgill, Henry, 104, 127
Tibetan Buddhists, 45-46, 51-53, 145,